A Rainbow Book

Photographing Beings of Light

Images of Nature...
...and Beyond

Orin Bridges

Rainbow Books, Inc.

Library of Congress Catalog Card Number — 93-83835

First Edition

ISBN: 1-56825-004-5

Cover Design: Betsy A. Lampé
Cover Production: Bonnie Rhodes
Cover Photo: "Dance of the Fairies," by Orin Bridges
Interior Design: Betsy A. Lampé

Published by Rainbow Books, Inc.
P. O. Box 430
Highland City, FL 33846-0430
Telephone (813) 648-4420

Manufactured in the United States of America

Dedication

This work is dedicated to all Beings of Light, whose presence is felt, whose energies sometimes appear on film, and whose unconditional love...is known.

Contents

Photo Index

Acknowledgments

Thanking the many persons who have encouraged me, in numerous, sometimes mysterious ways, to open to my gift of interdimensional photography is easy; naming all of them is nearly impossible, for many were catalysts, appearing at the right moment to utter a thought — or perhaps just a word — that I would recall months or even years later.

Some strangers appeared in my life to hasten the process, many of them unknown by name, some arriving to jolt me with an unpleasant encounter, frequently forcing me to make a reluctant decision. These decisions most often helped guide me on this veiled path I travel. Although I would not choose to repeat many of the experiences, I give my heartfelt thanks to these wonderful, though (in my perception then) harsh teachers.

I thank all persons whom you will meet in this book, acknowledging their important contribution, a contribution much greater than they would know in their conscious awareness, and although their name might be casually mentioned in passing, their presence in my life at that particular moment was no accident, and stands out in my memory as one of paramount significance.

Special thanks go to Michael, my wife, the wonderful woman who showed me, by example, how living things respond with love — when loved.

Introduction

Sales, marketing, real estate, financial planning, goal setting — this is how I might have defined "what I do" a few years back. None of these endeavors seem related, even remotely, to living in a harmonious way with Nature in a renewable energy home in the upper part of the Idaho panhandle, to becoming a vehicle through which the intelligences of Nature express their realness through what I term "interdimensional photography."

The "why me?" question still bubbles to the surface of my consciousness occasionally, followed swiftly with the "what next?" question. This entire episode of discovering my surprise gift — the ability to photograph other dimensional beings — gives credence to my oft-stated comment, "What I am doing has nothing to do with what I am doing."

It's hard to tell precisely when I made the decision to bring light into this dimension through photography, but I know the choice was made quite recently, since I didn't have the slightest interest in photography until 1988 when I bought my first "good" camera, and Light Beings began appearing in my photographs. My first thought was "camera problem!" but after all the potential mechanical failures were explored (several times) and found non-existent, I had two choices: accept the gift or deny it. Neither choice was easy for me.

The decision to use photography to assist us to elevate our consciousness, to expand our awareness, was not a conscious one; it was made at a higher level with the support and encouragement of many beings in the Devic Kingdom and other non-physical realities. I feel fortunate that through ongoing synchronistic events in my life I was made aware of being directed, even though the choices I made were cloaked in a garment of surprise.

Chapter 1

—The Beginnings—

R ecollections have a way of taking shape after the fact, the subconscious filling in the gaps, bringing forth pictures of happenings that the conscious mind chose to put into storage, happenings that may not be necessary or useful at the moment, but retained, not forgotten. So, my recollections, many in the forefront of memory, others conveniently being released as I recall the events, are telling this story, a true story, one that I still find both awesome and — in some strange way — expected.

There are at least two beginnings, the beginning that led up to the phenomenon I refer to as interdimensional photography, the second being the actual filming of Nature Spirits, Devic energies, the invisible intelligences.

The exact date of the first beginning is unknown by the conscious portion of my mind. But the recollection of events, like the replaying of a tape, allows me to pick up certain highpoints, peaks on a graph, standing out from the landscape of happenings, permitting these events to act as a landmark, a point of turning, a time when I changed course, chose a different path.

I now know that one of my purposes in my life plan, when I entered into this body, was to bring light into this dimension. There were, of course, many ways I could have done this; I could have been an artist, a composer, a writer, a film maker. But I feel I chose photography because it afforded me the closest thing to "proof" that invisible intelligences exist, and that through deductive logic — when all of the potential mechanical failures of the camera were explored and eliminated — the phenomenon becomes more acceptable, or at least is more seriously considered by those who come in contact with my work.

I chose photography as the vehicle, a method of expression, quite recently, not having the slightest interest in this method until 1988 when I bought my first "good" camera, and Light Beings began appearing in my photographs on the very first roll of film. The decision to use photography as a tool was not a conscious one; it was made at a higher level of consciousness with the support and encouragement of many beings in the Devic kingdom and in other non-physical realities. I was fortunate that through ongoing synchronistic events in my life, I was made aware of being directed, even though the choices I made were cloaked in a garment of surprise.

In 1955, my life's direction shifted — or at least the appearance of a shift registered in my conscious awareness — as the subtle synchronicity of daily "coincidences" began to mount, forming and/or identifying the path on which I would be, or am, traveling. The pivotal point was hearing a ten-inch, long-play record, a story narrated by Earl Nightingale titled, "The Strangest Secret."

In the record, Mr. Nightingale related his personal success story — how he was able to retire at age 35 by applying certain "secret" principles. I was impressed by the message the record conveyed; its appearance in my life seeming to be a part of the puzzle that I was trying to put together. I had often thought there was something beyond working and just "being here." And the "strangest secret," as Mr. Nightingale said, was not a secret at all. But by its very nature, since it wasn't a secret, was strange — strange because the message had been repeated in different words by some of the greatest thinkers and philosophers throughout all of recorded history; and still, 95 percent of the people who live on this planet did not consciously apply these principles.

The record's main point related to goal-setting, the process of establishing one's goals, introducing them into the subconscious and letting them flourish. Mr. Nightingale said the mind was like soil: You could plant a crop and the soil doesn't care whether you plant corn or deadly nightshade — it will produce whichever seed you plant in it. The choice is yours.

This thought fascinated me, and I reflected on the history of my life to that point, realizing that everything I had done, whether it was "good" or "bad," had transpired because I had chosen a path, and that most of my goal-setting in my early life had been done in a haphazard manner. I had chosen to be a person directed by forces outside of myself; and, in so doing, I had relinquished my turn at the helm, a captain sailing this vessel without charts, wondering why I kept running aground, unable to find my port and often blaming my crew — which consisted of whomever was at hand — for not arriving where I thought I should be.

After listening to that record day after day, copying it on tape and carrying it with me when I traveled, the idea of setting goals became paramount in my life, and goal-setting became my way of life. I set mostly monetary goals, money being so important to me at that time. I drew charts and graphs with time deadlines, dollar signs permeating the landscape of my goal plans, and found — true to what Mr. Nightingale said — that practically every goal I set was accomplished prior to the dates I had written on the charts. The one major exception was a five-year plan to become a millionaire, a plan that I intentionally aborted in 1962 in response to a needed release from the obsession with money.

At that time, I was going through a divorce, was suffering much guilt and confusion, and had temporarily returned to my old "why me?" mentality. In retrospect, it was clear that my ego was in full command, defending me from further harm by blocking, blinding and deafening me to the truth. The truth was that I had created every single happy — as well as unhappy — moment in my life.

In 1975, I was remarried and living in Escondido, California, was licensed in real estate, as well as being involved as an investor. I was an investor with little money — but with much creativity, thanks to many real estate professional exchangers from whom I learned and with whom I practiced.

It was in the late summer or early fall of that year that my wife Mike and I attended a lecture presented by the Nightingale-Conant group, a lecture to which we wouldn't have gone had I not made the connection with Earl Nightingale through his record, 20 years earlier. This "accidental" attendance at that evening seminar was one of the turning points that I remember with wonder and awe.

During the first part of the lecture, the speaker handed out cards, on which we were asked to write our goals and the date they were expected to materialize. My card read, "Have enough net worth to be able to retire in September 1978." It was an ambitious goal, since we were a great distance from any financial comfort-zone when we went to that meeting in June of 1975.

We didn't stay for the rest of the lecture, not realizing at the time that the only purpose of our going to that lecture was to write down this goal. I put the card in my wallet and didn't look at it again until September 13, 1978.

Almost immediately after moving to Escondido, we met and became good friends with our neighbors, Dave and Helen Glidden. We spent many weekends together barbecuing, exchanging dinners at home, going out for dinner, sharing thoughts, ideas, future plans, and listening to each other's dreams. It was during this early acquaintanceship that Dave and Helen talked about the cabin they had built at Lake Almanor, California, several hundred miles north of Escondido. We learned that the lake was nearly 5,000 feet above sea level, located in the mountains, and surrounded by beautiful scenery.

Each time they returned from their vacation home, they would show us photos of their cabin and the Lake Almanor area. Always full of enthusiasm, their vision of retiring there when they were able was uppermost in their minds, and more than once they made the suggestion that we should go to that area on vacation.

"It is so beautiful" Helen would say. "You really ought to see it,"

Little did we suspect that they would be a catalyst in helping us on our well-obscured path into the future.

But in the summer of 1978 we went on vacation to...Lake Almanor.

During our two-week vacation, we fell in love with the

Lake Almanor area, the tall, beautiful trees, the lake, the stillness, the people we met. Protected and shielded by its location, the area could have easily been a smaller version of Lake Tahoe. But it has been spared the commercial development because gambling wasn't legal, and there was no interstate highway system within 75 miles of this pristine, seemingly remote spot on the map.

During our first week at Lake Almanor, we were fishing from an old, rotten raft tied up on the east shore, and while reeling in a smallmouth bass, Mike said, "Do we really have to leave?"

She was unaware that I had done some financial projecting, trying to find a way to exit from the growing population density of the Escondido area, and longing for a more remote, natural place. I knew that if we were very frugal, if we really wanted to do it, we could manage it sometime within the next few years.

During our second week at the lake, we bought a lot in the Lake Almanor Country Club area, not because it was a country club, but because it was beautiful. Our plan was to build in another three years.

The lot was roughly one-half acre in size and was dense with towering fir trees that cast long shadows in the evening; and during the day, white cumulus clouds would move steadily across the blue sky, forming a backdrop against which the tall firs stretched their graceful, needled arms toward the sun. Deer wandered throughout the area, and due to their many generations of not being hunted, were unintimidated by humans at a safe distance.

The location seemed to have everything we had ever wanted. The property was within walking distance to the lake. Breathing the fresh, clear mountain air caused magical things to happen in our bodies' cellular structure; it opened our lungs, our heads and our hearts to the more important part of life...living it!

When we returned to Southern California, the three-years-future building date had miraculously compressed itself into a much shorter period. I immediately began drawing plans for our house, and I started thinking about selling some of the real estate we had acquired, including our residence. So, we started to advertise and distributed the property information through the exchange groups.

Things kept falling into place, as if unseen hands and minds were somehow busy at work making sure there would be no delay; the whole transition was a flowing, near-effort-less event. People arrived, like actors in our play, on a precise, split-second cue. Buyers for our properties materialized, as if they had been waiting in the wings of our theater, their lines memorized with impeccable accuracy, knowing just how much to offer, what terms we would accept and when escrow would close.

Due to my association with what I believed was the most creative group of real estate people ever assembled on this earth, and having absorbed these creative energies, then expanding them into my own aura of creativity, the disposition of our properties was like being involved in a life-sized Monopoly game. Nearly all of our holdings, including our personal residence, were transferred to new owners almost immediately in a mysterious, guided manner. It was much too smooth to be "normal."

During this same period of whirlwind "rightness," I sublet my office, sold my office furniture and we had our Lake Almanor home built by Randy Broglio, who had been recommended by Dave and Helen. Dave and Helen had enjoyed a good relationship with Randy during the construction of their home at the lake. Randy, in his conscientious manner, had our home completed enough for us to move in on December 23, 1978, just six months from the time we took our vacation at Lake Almanor to "see what it was like!"

My birthday in September 1978 was a special event. Mike decided to ask the Gliddens over for dinner, both to celebrate my birthday and our "retirement."

Dave and Helen must have had mixed emotions on that evening. On one hand, they were thrilled that we were able to move to the area they loved. But on the other hand, we were being separated by 800 miles, and it had been *their* long-term goal to retire there as soon as possible.

Mike cooked a wonderful dinner, and the four of us were

in a festive mood, enjoying a beautiful evening, sharing hopes and expectations. And as dinner was completed, a small box appeared in front of me, along with a birthday card from Mike. Before I opened it, I almost knew the gift was a replacement for my overused wallet, a wallet stuffed with credit cards and little notes, insurance identification, Social Security card and other items. As I removed the wrapping paper, I smelled the leather; then as the inner wrapping of tissue paper was peeled away, I saw the new brown wallet.

At that time in my life, I thought I needed all of these credit cards, the Social Security card and other little pieces of paper that I was now transferring to the new wallet — much of it not having seen the light of day for months or more. Toward the bottom of the stack of cards that I removed, a small item caught my attention. It was a printed card with something written on it, something I had completely forgotten. It was the "goals" card that I had put in my wallet over three years ago — put there and not once uncovered, not once looked at since the Nightingale-Conant meeting in June of 1975, but the goal had still materialized, with no (conscious) effort! "Have enough net worth by September 1978 to retire," stood out, bolder than bold, on this card. Our little birthday and retirement gathering took place on September 13, 1978.

During the construction period, things moved almost as smoothly as the sale of our properties in Southern California. I decided to do the electrical wiring myself, even though I had never before done it. I bought a Sunset "how-to" book, and with a fair knowledge of electricity extending back to my junior high school days, I diagrammatically laid out the wiring; and with some guidance from Randy, I was able to understand what I needed to know about the electrical code.

Randy's wife Paige wished me luck when she learned that I had never wired a house before, that I was armed only with a Sunset book and determination. As it turned out, no luck was needed. The rough-in inspection passed without any changes.

I think Randy was more relieved than I when Bob, the building inspector, said in a serious tone, "I have some news for you, Orin — it's going to work!"

During construction, our temporary residence consisted of an 8 by 20 foot travel trailer, hooked up to the septic system and the community water supply. This particular phase of the building project didn't go quite as well as it could have. The plumbing froze up — not just the incoming water, but the shower drain, the kitchen drain and the everything drain — and civilized living came to a standstill. It seemed I was always driving to town for propane, and we were always running out of heat during the coldest nights. This was not in the plan. Awakening during the night to the strange crashing sounds of some wild animal (most likely a deer) stumbling across the stacked lumber wasn't in the plan, either.

But prior to that, in the early fall when we started construction, our evenings were spent in appreciation of the area and of our home, which was rapidly taking shape. Each evening, when the workers left, we would climb to the main floor via a ladder, Mike doing her best to overcome her acrophobia. We would sit on a pile of lumber and enjoy a glass of wine, reflect on our move and look forward to our future here, at Lake Almanor. An owl greeted us almost every evening, perching above us in a giant white fir. Our two dogs, having been raised in suburban neighborhoods, were ecstatic in their new environment. Our (mostly) beagle, Stretch, with her nose to the ground, and Wiley, our other multi-breed, with nose in the air, both dogs' tails wagging, explored the new smells of the forest daily, their acute senses tuned to the peak of reception.

Each evening, we would leash our dogs and take them into their new "neighborhood," which consisted of mostly woods, with an occasional house visible from the road. On one occasion, during a warm fall evening, we left the trailer door open, walked the dogs for about half an hour and returned after dark. The dogs were, as usual, excited about their outing, and as we came around the end of the trailer, we spotted an animal directly in front of our open door, its tail raised and looking over its shoulder at us. It was a skunk!

We immediately turned around, the dogs obediently following on their leashes as we commanded them to "Come on!" The four of us retreated from the trailer area, and Mike and I felt grateful that the dogs were leashed and didn't choose to jump our skunk visitor. After we had gone about 50 feet, we discovered that Wiley was unhooked from her leash. We didn't know it — she didn't know it.

All of our dogs' future encounters with skunks were not quite as uneventful, unfortunately, so we maintained an ample supply of tomato juice and other assorted items to help neutralize — but not totally eliminate — the skunk odor buried deep in their coats.

Retirement is, in my definition, doing what you want to do, when you want to do it. By this definition, then, I really retired at Lake Almanor, even though after a short period of time I became active once again in real estate exchanging, started an exchange group in the county, acquired properties, wrote and presented continuing education real estate seminars throughout California and Nevada for about five years, and continued to act in a very unretired manner. But none of these activities occurred during our first year.

It took some time to get acquainted with our new surroundings, make the usual "flatlander" mistakes, become acclimated to living at a 5,000 foot elevation, and do stuff around the house. For the first year, we did not see television, subscribe to a newspaper, and we had finally shifted completely from the Southern California "busy mode" to one of a more relaxed pattern.

We traveled to our nearest town, Chester, fairly often to pick up groceries, visit the library and purchase what was needed. Mike enjoyed our shopping visits, but they wore me out. So, we came to a kind of unspoken agreement that she would go alone, except when we shopped for groceries. On one of her solo trips to Chester, she bought me a book.

Mike knew that I was not a reader in the sense she was. I rarely read fiction, no longer needed to keep up with business trends and financial markets, and I felt uninterested in political stuff. In short, I didn't feel much like reading anything, and Mike knew it. Why, then, would she bring me this book, a thick book at that, titled *Seth Speaks*, hand it to me and say, "You might like it"...? This non-coincidence was too extraordinary to ignore.

Seth Speaks, by Jane Roberts, preceded the now almost common phenomenon of channeling. It dealt with Jane's confusion and understandable concern when she connected with a different reality through Seth, a non-physical being, and then began to channel information. Seth was an abstract, wordy, philosophical, entertaining and instructive teacher, causing my mind to stretch and expand in a multidirectional fashion.

My perception was that each of his paragraphs could be assigned to a weekly study group for interpretation and reflection. The book Mike brought home, because she "thought I would like it," was the beginning of the exponential growth of our metaphysical interests. *Seth Speaks* was followed by other *Seth* books, channeled by Jane Roberts, which were followed by the use of the ouija board, ESP cards and other books all more and more varied, interesting and mystical.

After we had been at Lake Almanor for about three years, we were able to acquire a lake-front lot where we would build another home, not just walking distance to water, but *on the lake*. In the summer of 1984, we built our second Lake Almanor home, this one a manifestation of Mike's dream, her dream of being on the water. I designed the house with a great amount of glass on the south side, facing the lake. The kitchen looked out on the lake, so Mike could more fully enjoy cooking; the living area looked out at the lake, a sliding glass door opened out onto the deck; the master bedroom had another glass slider which opened onto a portion of the lakeside deck; Mike's baby grand Yamaha piano also had a lake view from its location at the rear of the living area; and even my office, at the ground level, faced the lake. This house would not be comfortable anywhere else. Make no mistake, it was a house for lake living, and Mike's dream had come true.

Like all pianos, especially after they have been moved, Mike's Yamaha needed to be tuned. Even I could tell that the Bach pieces didn't sound quite right as Mike practiced, and Mike, being the accomplished musician that she is, was keenly aware that a piano doctor was required to bring her friend back to health.

The Yellow Pages listed Syd Allen of Westwood as the closest piano tuner. Mike called him, neither of us remotely connecting that casual, simple decision to another adventure.

Syd arrived at our home at 10:00 or 11:00 in the morning, tuning paraphernalia in hand. He introduced himself to us, to the piano, and he went to work. As he tuned, his eyes drifted to the shelf under the coffee table where our ouija board rested. "Do you folks use that very often?" he asked, speaking in the code of the metaphysical underground.

"Once is a while," Mike replied, also speaking in code.

"We have a little group..." Syd started out. He then explained, as the conversation moved from the guarded to the more open, that we were welcome to join them at their next meeting.

How interesting, we both thought, that this introduction should occur in such an "accidental manner."

The first meeting was a week from the time we spoke to Syd. As we entered this Westwood home, we were warmly greeted by Syd's wife Gerri, who introduced us to the others. The feeling of kinship with all those present was immediate. We were encouraged to explore our own psychic abilities, to understand that we all possess the gifts that we sometimes consider exclusively belonging to others. We psychometrized things, each of us privately wrapping an object in tissue paper, putting it in a bowl, then each person having an opportunity to "read" the object through the paper. It was an incredible introduction to this small group and to our own personal power. There were eight of us, and every person was able to read a least a partial vibrational impression left on the subject by the owner or former owner of the item.

At future meetings, we took a meditation trip to the inner earth, psychometrized a map for its power points, took an etheric space craft trip to Mount Shasta and brought back similar but unexpected images. We had what I now refer to as "metaphunsical" experiences.

The Lake Almanor area enjoyed all of earth's four seasons. Each season was uniquely beautiful, and our biological clocks seemed to be in tune with the changes each season brought about. Winter, detested by many who live in wintry climates, was an enjoyable experience, and the first year we spent in the snow we became children again. We built a toboggan run on the vacant lot next to ours; we got wet and cold, and we laughed at ourselves, our dogs and the world. The snow fell straight down, sometimes in giant flakes, covering the earth and all of her vegetation that had gone to rest until spring, when Mother Earth would call, once again, to come out and play. There were seldom snow drifts like I remembered as a child growing up in Michigan, which my memory connected as an inseparable part of winter. But the sun shone, reflecting light into our lives, our cells, our bodies, our spirits, and we rejoiced.

We noticed the winters were even brighter when we moved to our new lake-front home; the sunlight flowed, almost unrestricted, across the lake's cold surface, and through the few trees that towered above the deck on the southern face of the house. Our 325-foot driveway led to the snowplowed road, which led out of the country club. We purchased a used snowblower to insure wintertime mobility.

As we attended more metaphysical meetings, read more books, our awareness of many things increased. I became convinced of how my thoughts — very often unconscious ones — controlled my perception of life. The snowblower became the vehicle, in one memorable instance, that allowed me to become aware of my passing thoughts, thoughts that I normally allowed to flow through me, that would unconsciously become guides for my actions and reactions.

It was one of those wonderful sun-bright days, the sky was completely clear without even one of those frequently seen puffy clouds which often stenciled white images onto the sky. It was nature's crystal blue ceiling. During this stage of — I guess you would call it "awakening" — I was not aware of the importance of light in our bodies and in our lives, but I felt like I was almost breathing light. It was a glorious day, and I was snow-blowing.

As I made the first return pass from the road to our garage, and about halfway down the slight hill, I consciously thought, What a beautiful day to be alive, here in this location, at this wonderful moment! Immediately, another thought arrived from my subconscious, one totally unexpected, but revealing:

You can't enjoy this yet.

I stopped the thought before it passed out of range. Wait a minute, I almost said out loud. Why can't I enjoy this day?

Because you haven't yet finished your job.

Here I was, in complete joy and in harmony with the events and the experiences of the day, and I was telling myself that I couldn't be "rewarded" until later, when all was complete. It was like "enlightenment can wait until the snow is cleared." Then I remembered what Seth had said in one of his books about core beliefs. He drew the analogy that our beliefs are like furniture in an attic, that we can enter the attic, examine what is there, then choose to move the furniture around, discard it, replace it, or keep it — it's up to us. This seemed like the very first visit to my mental attic.

As our association with the wonderful members of the small group intensified; I seemed to be the only one of us who was drawn to the Ramtha audio tapes, tapes that arrived in our mailbox from a friend in Southern California. Ramtha was an entity channeled by J. Z. Knight of Washington state. He was an entity that I believed to be a great teacher. I seemed to be almost compelled to listen to his tapes, hour after hour, absorbing the messages of unconditional love, reminding us that we are all gods, encouraging us to see that same quality in all humans. In his early dissertations, his speech was interspersed with East Indian phrases, like "As it were indeed," speaking with a decided accent; so, it took concentration to hear the complete message.

How great it would be if he had videos, I mused, or to be in the audience.

At about this time, it was becoming more clear to our conscious minds that much was transpiring in the invisible realms that affected our thinking/acting processes in this reality. We knew that "somewhere out there," a great deal of cooperation was going on, our higher selves interacting with others in such an interwoven manner that it would defy

explanation. Now, the subtle suggestions, feelings and urgings were filtering down through my layers of logic, and after
our group (etheric) space-craft journey to Mount Shasta,
four of us — Syd and his wife Gerri, Mike and I — decided to
take another trip to the mountain...but this time it would be
a physical trip. Just a casual trip, mind you.

We arrived at the Golden Boughs Bookstore in Mount
Shasta just as the owner arrived to open for business. While
Dorothy, the owner, went about the things all store owners
do when they open, we started to browse, and I picked up a
small booklet on learning how to channel. I laid it on the
counter, preparing to pay for it with other items we would
purchase, but Dorothy handed it to me and explained it was
a gift. That was strange enough, since I had never before met
Dorothy. But when I looked at the printing on this booklet, I
saw, for the first time, the name of the personality that had
been channeled by Sanaya Roman, the author. The name of
the entity was "Orin!" This was the beginning of a day of
synchronicity so bizarre and unreal that, when I returned
home, I went to my word processor and listed these events
chronologically. The list of "coincidences" exceeded a single-
spaced, typewritten page.

Within a few minutes, Dorothy had put a Ramtha audio
tape into her tape system, and it was playing when another
person entered the bookstore, a man with whom I connected
immediately. As he and I both moved toward the shelf where
the Ramtha books were on display, we began to exchange
opinions concerning the teachings of Ramtha. Within the
first few moments of our conversations, he turned to me and
said, "The videos are really great."

"Videos?" I queried.

"Yes, videos," he replied, obviously surprised I hadn't
heard of them.

"And," said Dorothy of the bookstore, overhearing our
conversation, "I have them." She offered to rent them to us for
a very reasonable amount.

My logical mind went into overtime trying to figure that
one out. First, we were drawn to Mount Shasta, then to the
bookstore, then to the stranger, and now we discovered that,

not only do Ramtha videos exist, but Dorothy has them, was willing to rent them to us — complete strangers from over 100 miles away — with no deposit or identification required.

Shortly after the Mount Shasta visit, the attendance at our metaphysical group meetings shifted dramatically. We bought and shared Ramtha videos, at which time new people arrived at the meetings. Some of the "regulars" stopped attending, even though they had never seen the first Ramtha video, clearly indicating that their guidance chose to keep them away, obviously not to be involved in Ramtha's teaching for reasons that were their very own; but, new visitors were being called to join us in this experience. It was fascinating to watch this process of discernment at work.

After we viewed the first Ramtha video, Syd expressed his feeling that there was something more than what we saw and heard, something beyond audio and visual impressions. We unanimously agreed that there seemed to be an intangible "something" included on the tape. Subsequent tapes, all of them, seemed to transmit, in addition to the visual images and the sound, an underlying vibrational tone that was at the feeling level.

Recently, I came to the conclusion that this consists of the combined, projected electromagnetic energy of all persons involved in the process: the teachers, instructors or persons being video taped; the technicians, camera operators, musicians who produce the score; the director, producer and all others who are contributing in any way to the finished product. This is not limited to the Ramtha videos, but, in my perception, this vibrational tone becomes an integral part of all videos. If we are in resonance with the particular frequencies infused in the tape, we will be drawn to that video and, conversely, if our frequency is out of phase with the frequencies embedded within the video, we will not be open to them. The realization of this principal came to me several years later, during the 1991 Body, Mind, Spirit and Earth EXPO held in Seattle, Washington, where I was an exhibitor.

One of the Ramtha tapes that we viewed in early 1987 was about earth changes. Although, from a truly historical perspective Ramtha was a much better teacher than a prophet, this tape filled my mind with the thought of more self-reliance, more independence, a need for the recognition of my sovereignty. The fact that we lived in the shadow of Mount Lassen, a (dormant?) volcano, gave credulity to my beliefs about the high-risk area of Lake Almanor. My inner self was providing me with all the reasons needed to move. My left brain insisted that we relocate, offering more and more "logical" reasons to leave our new home on the lake, to separate ourselves by hundreds of miles from our friends and family, to depart from the comfort level we were just getting used to. These thoughts, that were being introduced into my conscious thought processes, were now demanding recognition and action.

All the reasons — I discovered later — were not reasons at all, but excuses, excuses to move from this two-year-old home situated on the lake front to four acres at the end of an Idaho road, a rutted Idaho road at that, where we knew no one and where we would have to build another home.

There is no doubt in my mind that my higher self knew it had to feed my logical mind with justifications in order to get me to make this move to northern Idaho, to where I *had* to be. All the reading I did, the seminars I went to, the political climate in the country club where we lived, all — in some manner — contributed to the state of mind that cried out for a change, a move. I felt it was imperative to be more self-sufficient in a rural setting, to have our own well water pumped by a source of energy that didn't depend on an outside supplier, to grow our own vegetables (although my gardening experience was woefully lacking), to have most of the umbilical cords of utilities cut. These were practical goals I had always nurtured, I told myself. But in reflecting on these goals — if indeed they existed — I surmised that they had to be buried deep in my subconscious. So deep, in fact, that I am now more inclined to accept it as a manufactured rationale.

One of the last in a series of events prior to our move was my running for the board of directors of the country club. It is hilarious, in retrospect, to see how I became so embroiled in — as I perceived it then — the conspiracy of the golfers and other establishment individuals to force the rest of us into supporting the amenities we never used. My perception also allowed me to see the problems clearly. Since the dues went up every year, the average homeowner was not represented, more and more restrictions were placed on our little community by the board of directors, and it was really time for a change to a more fiscally responsible management.

That wasn't enough, however. In addition, the restrictions of the club prevented us from drilling our own well, the water system was in a sad state of repair, our dependency on electric pumps to fill the storage tanks made us totally dependent on the utility company that also owned the lake, our roads were not maintained by the county and were in serious need of repair, and the list went on.

I managed to become confrontational enough to lose the election, and when the votes were tallied, my higher self breathed a sigh of relief, and for good reason, for if I had won that non-paying directorship — the campaign rivaling a state senatorial race in political rhetoric and denunciations — I would have been committed to stay there for two or three more years. I find it intriguing that, without my great leadership ability, the country club has managed to survive. Hard to believe.

The timing of our move seemed critical, like there was some sort of cosmic timetable that I was following. I felt a great urgency in relocating. But where? We had a choice of going almost anywhere in the U.S. So, what location, what area, state or region would be the place to move? It obviously wasn't a question of a beautiful environment — we were already enjoying one that would be difficult to duplicate, one that had all the natural beauty we desired. The self-sufficiency rationale kept revolving in my consciousness. Land was important, land that had no utilities that would have to be depended upon, land that would not be a part of a structured subdivision. The location would have to have a less intrusive political environment, a place where we could be more in concert with our surroundings, a place where the inner urges would be satisfied. I was unaware that the location, like the timing, seemed to already be a part of the probable future.

During this period of — I won't call it unrest, more like preparation — I was still behaving in a very unretired way. But, the mysterious timetable became easier to follow as obligation after obligation melted away. As the time came closer to move, a small barter group that I had started conveniently died a natural death due to lack of interest by the business community and the small geographical area of coverage. The real estate lectures became less profitable due to the state's acceptance of home study courses in addition to personally attended classes for continued education credits.

The "problem properties" that I owned suddenly became desirable for the right owners, the negative cash flow with which I had lived for many — oh, so many years — turning into positive cash flow. The right people arrived at the right time to assist in disassembling any notions I may have had that I was in a tight spot. Everything was going according to "the plan," whatever that was. A familiar pattern began emerging, the pattern that strongly resembled our move from Escondido to Lake Almanor.

It would be misleading of me to say that all things went well prior to and during our next transition — the move from Lake Almanor to Idaho. The timetable went well, as did the disposition of properties which freed us of some obligations and resulted in additional income. All the physical events went smoothly, except for one thing: Mike didn't want to leave Lake Almanor.

Mike loves water, loved her lake-front dream home, and had acquired some close friends in that small community. But, once again, she was being asked to uproot, to move to another location — 800 miles away.

Mike would miss her walks along the lake's shore with our dogs, the sound of the lake as it spoke softly to her on summer nights, the families of Canadian geese and their goslings swimming the shallows in front of our home, the ospreys as they circled overhead with their catch, the bald eagles perching in the nearby snag, the beach activities in the summertime. She would miss all of this and more, much more.

This was a very stressful time for Mike. The thought of leaving hurt her deeply, emotionally torn between wanting to stay, enjoying the life she was now living, and going north to please me. At the same time, I was so determined to move, to go to that state called "sovereign," that my feelings took on the appearance of uncaring resolution. My unswerving course made me tunnel-visioned, singular in direction and focus. I would not let myself see how she was being wrenched, and subconsciously I knew that if I allowed the doubts of the proposed move to become part of my daily thought processes, the move itself would be jeopardized, and my determination would be awash in re-evaluation and self-doubt. If this had taken place, the move would have been aborted.

I have since allowed myself to realize how she was torn, how difficult it was for her during and after this move, how extremely trying it was for this strong, beautiful person. The difficult commitment and decision she made to support me in this endeavor cannot be minimized. Her determined love, her nurturing instincts, her balanced and centered attitude have been the stabilizing factor in many of our adventures, both before and after our move to Idaho.

As soon as the election in the country club was over, we found ourselves taking trips to various locations in various states. We drove to Michigan, to Colorado, to Washington, looking at properties, and found, without exception, logical reasons why these locations were not right for us: an inadequate supply of good water; too much rain; too little rain; rocky terrain; too windy; prices out of reach. I was the one who insisted on a south slope, a good well, the right price and terms. The logical reasons seemed to best fit my department, while Mike operated more from a right-brain perspective. But after all the evaluating, weighing, judging, outlining and summarizing, the final decision was dependent upon the "feel" for the area, the land. The left brain, with great reluctance, had to step aside in this process.

One of our trips included a seminar in Seattle, a Ramtha seminar, a seminar on manifesting. Sharri, a friend of ours from the Lake Almanor area and a frequent visitor at our little group meetings, traveled with us. During the visualization process, guided by Ramtha, I saw with my inner vision the right property with a small structure on it: south slope, plenty of water, remote. It was what I had in mind, naturally. The seminar was scheduled for two days, but it lasted more like a day and a half, so we three were able to leave during daylight hours and drive toward Idaho. We arrived the next day and spent that night with Bobbie in Coeur d'Alene. Bobbie and her children were relatives of Mike's, the only people we knew in the state of Idaho.

The next day, Roger, a friend of Bobbie's suggested we might drive up to Sandpoint. "The consciousness level is even higher than the poverty level," he joked.

"Where is Sandpoint," we asked.

"Fifty miles north, near Canada."

Seems like we were being nudged again.

We drove north.

Chapter 2

—Appointment With
the Future—

I f you were to follow Highway 95 north, through Sandpoint, you would cross the Canadian border in about an hour's drive and enter the province of Alberta. Much of the border crossing in this vicinity, from south to north and from north to south, is done by near-border residents; U.S. citizens visiting Canada to enjoy a week-end of relaxing in hot springs, visiting Banff National Park, Lake Louise or still further north, Jasper National Park; and Canadians coming to Sandpoint to shop, to vacation in the summertime, and to ski Mount Schweitzer during the winter season. On the U.S. side of the border, it is not uncommon to see signs posted in merchant's windows and on motels which advertise "Canadian at par," meaning the Canadian dollar will be accepted at face value, which, in effect, offers a discount of 15 percent to 20 percent to our Canadian visitors, due to the difference in the value of the dollars.

The Sandpoint City limits sign reads: "Pop. 5200." But during the summer, the town appears to grow by at least ten times that number as visitors arrive for various events. K-Mart recently built a new, large store just outside the city limits, McDonald's golden arches have maintained their high visibility north of town for quite a few years, as has Pizza Hut on the opposite side of the street. A quick check of the license plates at any one of these locations will quickly convince the curious that Sandpoint is the hub of something or other, with Canada, Washington state and Montana strongly represented. But if one looks at a map, it becomes apparent that Sandpoint is located at about the skinniest part of the panhandle with only 65 highway miles separating the states of Washington and Montana, and an easy drive for many

Canadians.

On our first visit, we both felt right about the Sandpoint area, and in speaking to many others who have settled here, the immediate *feel* of the area was one of the factors that contributed to their decision to take up residence. The people we met on our first visit were genuine, friendly, helpful, unpretentious, making an outsider feel welcome, and for a small town it has an abundance of activities. The Spokane Symphony and well known performers personally appear for the Sandpoint Festival in late summer, and a large contingent of artists, musicians and other creative individuals choose to make their home in or around Sandpoint. My eldest son refers to Sandpoint as "the Carmel of the Northwest."

Beautiful scenery is a part of the region: mountain meadows colorfully responding to the call of spring; streams, some seasonal, some year around, bringing clear, cold water from the snow run-off to the rivers and lakes below; wilderness areas, horse trails, hiking trails, deer trails. Moose, bear, hard-to-see cougars, coyotes, fox, and many other smaller mammals and birds, make their homes here.

The town of Sandpoint lives up to its name, situated on a point of land extending into Lake Pend Oreille (pronounced Ponderay). Pend Oreille River, ideal for water skiing, fishing, sailing and swimming, runs from the lake in a westerly direction into the state of Washington, joining and becoming the mighty Columbia, where it continues its long journey to the Pacific Ocean. Mount Sweitzer, a large and growing ski resort, overlooks the city, and the community is awash with events, summer and winter. Art shows, craft shows, bicycle races, a three-state triathalon, walkathons, and activities designed to appeal to most any interest or ability, as a participant or spectator, are ongoing. And it's less than two hours from a fairly large city, Spokane, Washington.

Mike and I have never discussed what she tried to manifest during the exercises Ramtha led us through when we were in his seminar in Seattle. I visualized a parcel of land with a south slope, lots of water, good soil and trees on the north side. In my experience, visualized events and places seldom come into form in the exact manner that they were visualized, perhaps relating to my inability to see them during the visualization process with the utmost clarity. But since the "wants" in this case were fairly basic, I surmised it shouldn't be too hard for the Universe to create. Perhaps if I had asked for the property to be at a specific elevation, located on a certain section of land, including a species of trees not normally found in northern Idaho, with a sizable deposit of gold on the property, it may have taken a little longer to manifest.

It seemed both unreal, and at the same time normal, to be looking for property in this area, just a few months after our first introduction to the teachings and prophesies of Ramtha. It was a forceful reminder that we do, in fact, choose and create our own realities, and the choice we were making was an immense one. But throughout the selection process, the choice seemed very natural, non-threatening and adventuresome.

At our meetings at Lake Almanor, the group purpose was to explore, expand and entertain our consciousness; meditation began the meetings, meditation ended the meetings, and our discussion topics were as varied as the persons attending. Most often, the agenda — if you chose to call it that — was open, following our feelings. Discussions were always filled with interest and much intuitive guidance. Once in a while, an individual would discuss an event or book, sometimes outlining its contents, sometimes recommending it to others. Personal experiences were shared and, although there were no rules, personal situations, sometimes called problems, were rarely, if ever, discussed. So when I found myself relating the events that caused my partnership properties to become burdens, I wondered why I was doing this, why I was talking about personal, financial things — but I kept right on talking.

This meeting was in the spring of 1986, and I was obviously unaware that one of my core beliefs was that *events directed my life*, rather than the events were a manifestation of those beliefs. During my dissertation, everyone listened patiently to my story about the "events" that caused my stressful financial position, causing me to lose a property, in debt with no relief in sight. I had conveniently forgotten the real estate exchangers frequently repeated phrase, "There are no problem properties — just inappropriate ownership," but I continued on, seemingly compelled to continue this saga, ignoring my mental reminder that this was, after all, a metaphysical gathering, not a financial board meeting.

After I had talked some time about these situations, which seemed like overwhelming burdens, there was a short silence, and then Gerri said simply, "Look how powerful you are." It would be two years before I knew the meaning of that comment.

It is intriguing that those five words, "Look how powerful you are," would stay with me, intact, unaltered, unmodified, unforgotten, for that period of time. It is clear (now) that the words were buried in my subconscious until I was prepared to alter my perception and adopt a greater understanding and acceptance of a gradual, but evolving philosophy within my being.

After we had moved into our new home in Idaho, the real meaning became clear: We *are* powerful. So powerful, in fact, that we create, or co-create, every crisis as well as every happiness, every joy, every sadness, every victory, every defeat, every event in our lives. The scenario that I perceived as negative — and it was financially negative — was created by *me*, just as surely as the one that followed, which led me *out* of the financial difficulties I was concerned about and into a clearer understanding of my own abilities, beliefs and attitudes which shape my life. It dawned on me, two years later, what Gerri really meant. She was saying that it takes just as much power to create a problem as it does to create a solution, and that I was/am a powerful being, as we *all* are.

It was no mistake that *this* scene appeared in *this* act of *my* play. I wrote Gerri and thanked her.

Although we both agreed on the area, our preferences as to the lifestyle differed considerably. I would just as soon have been in the backwoods five miles from the nearest house, but Mike wanted to be closer to people. We looked at some properties I liked, but Mike felt she would have to be "airlifted out once a week," since some of these parcels were really remote. Then, there was the one that we *both* liked, south of Sandpoint. But the water supply was questionable, since it had no well drillers' report on file, and I had a big thing about having ample water. This property *did* have a south slope, good soil, and trees on the north side, just like I had visualized.

One family with two different, and opposing, needs didn't make it easy on the real estate agent. Here was this couple: The man, willing to settle in the backwoods and be snowed in all winter if necessary, and the lady who wanted to be near town. We were driven around a lot, while the sales person tried to find some kind of a compromise property. To make it more difficult, since I felt an abundance of water was important, I had insisted on a well that would pump 30 gallons per minute. Had I been privy to the evening conversations in the agent's home, the conversation would undoubtedly have included such words as "California dreamers," "unrealistic," "survivalists," and "impossible."

One of the things that made the area so appealing to me was the friendly manner in which the building departments and affiliated inspection people operated, and, until 1977, there were, in fact, no building permits required. But at the same time, I wished that well drillers' reports *had* been a requirement, since what made the water part of the property-selection process even more complex was the lack of well drillers' reports on most of the properties, showing the wells' maximum rates of flow.

On our second visit — after we had pretty much exhausted our choices and the realtor's patience — one of the agents came into the office with a property listing less than six miles from town, at the end of a road, and with a livable cabin on it. The cabin, he said, had been built by a former owner and was in impeccable condition. It included two solar panels, two deep-cycle storage batteries, a septic system, a 500-gallon cistern and a well that would deliver *60 gallons per minute!* When I heard about the water supply, "too good to be true" popped into my head. Did that phrase represent my belief? Why should anything be untrue because it's good? Maybe it's time to search the attic again, Orin, and discard

those old pieces of furniture, those outmoded, useless say-
ings and beliefs. Too good to be true, indeed!

Within minutes after learning of this offering, we found
ourselves seated in a couple of four-wheel drive vehicles,
heading west through Dover, a small community easily
overlooked except for the slower speed limit which allowed us
to see the only public building, the post office, situated in an
old house right on the highway. As we resumed highway
speed, we drove over a railroad overpass, followed the river
for two miles, then turned north onto a graveled easement
road.

The first one-fourth mile up the hill was relatively easy
going, but that changed as we turned left into the woods. As
we drove this bumpy, rutted road, there were no houses,
fences, power lines, phone lines or other signs of life. It was
definitely private. After another one-half mile, the easement
road turned right, but we continued straight, passed a log
cabin that was barely visible through the trees on the right,
and then entered a long, tree-lined lane that crossed over a
small rise.

The date was December 12th, but the weather was just
about at the freezing mark, which I considered fairly mild for
so near Canada. The sun was shining, reflecting off the light
sprinkling of snow in the open areas around the cabin. The
four-wheel drives would not have been needed that day, but
as the real estate agents reminded us, "break-up" would
make the access road next to impassable, so we should
consider a "four by four" if we decided to live here.

"Spring break-up" is when the frost comes out of the
ground as the earth thaws, turning the dirt roads in the area
into mush, bogging down many vehicles, including four-
wheel drives, if the vehicles sink to their axles in this bottom-
less mud. During the break-up period, the state highway
department imposes load and speed limits for logging and
other trucks to prevent serious damage to the highways. But
even with this precaution, Nature has its way, and it is a
common sight to see highway workers every spring, patching
the "frost heaves" wrought by the power of freeze-thaw
conditions.

I couldn't get over the 60 gallons per minute quoted by the realtor. Was this the owner's estimate? Was it a deep well? Was the 60 gallons per minute for just *one* minute and then it went dry? Was there a well driller's report? The answers, we soon learned, were no, yes, no and yes. The well was 325 feet deep, and the well driller's report showed it *did* deliver 60 gallons per minute! A 30-gallon-per-minute well was next to impossible to find, according to our limited, but concentrated experience in the area, so a 60 gpm well had to be next to a miracle. Maybe a coincidence?

The present owner, who lived there alone and hand pumped the well water, had installed a 1000-gallon septic system, added a bathroom to the cabin, and kept the area in immaculate condition. The cabin, which faced south, sat pretty much in the center of an approximate one-acre meadow. The remainder of the 4.2 acres was covered with jack pine, birch, cedar, tamarack, and a scattering of grand fir and white pine. The closest parcel of neighboring land, south of the cabin, consisted of 17 acres that had some serious drawbacks for building in the vicinity of our land, which made the property more or less a buffer zone. To the west was another parcel that could not be built on, the northerly parcel was separated from this acreage by a small ravine, and to the east, the log cabin that we passed, entering this property, was removed from our view and was occupied by a school teacher and his wife.

When we drove over the small knoll entering the property from the east, there was no question — *this was it!* This was *our* property, would be our new home. It was *more* than the snow reflecting the winter sun, it was *more* than the cabin being so well cared for, *more* than it was at the end of a road, or that we were tired of looking. It was close enough to matching my visualization to cause my "wonder and awe" state to kick in. It was right!

We entered the cabin, and it was all the real estate listing said it was, and more. Birch cabinets, even in this rustic setting. The stairs that led to the loft, the drawers and storage cabinets below the stairwell, were all crafted from cherry wood. The original owner, we learned, had moved to Alaska, but when in Idaho he had owned a small business dealing in specialty woods.

Bob, the present owner of the land, was a geologist who frequently traveled to Canada on assignment, using the cabin on his stays in the Sandpoint area. He had installed a long-handled pump in the pumphouse and had added counterbalancing weights to make the pumping easier. To deliver the pumped water to the cistern, located underground next to the cabin, he had installed 125 feet of PVC pipe between the pumphouse and the storage tank, buried about a foot below ground level. The six-foot drop between theses two locations allowed gravity to clear the pipe of any standing water, eliminating any potential winter freeze problems.

"Pumping water is good exercise," he assured me.

I discovered he was right, as I did it for quite some time before I devised my own 12-volt system of pumping water.

After we inspected the cabin, we walked out in the meadow and looked at the land. If we added on to the cabin, we would only have to cut down a couple of trees and the house could be oriented to true south, facing the meadow. We could have a garden on the south slope in full view of the house, and the solar panels could be mounted on the roof, furnishing the needed solar power to charge the batteries that would provide our electricity. The house could be designed with the living/dining areas facing south, joined by a sun space that would collect and store heat from the winter sun, hopefully reducing our dependency on firewood to heat the house.

The cabin was impressive, no doubt about it. But the land, well, there was more to it than just land. There was a certain *feel* to it, a certain hard-to-describe peacefulness, almost like a place we visited before, a place that had changed, but somehow still remained the same, a place where the soul could rest.

Little did I know that the feeling I was experiencing, that ripple of recognition that ran through my body, was a communication. Little did we know that the beings of the earth were there awaiting our arrival, that our lives would be forever changed the moment we stepped foot in this magical space, that the Devic Kingdom was just a mind's blink away. No *conscious* knowledge, that is.

The silence of this December morning was disturbed only by our voices and the occasional call of a raven in the nearby woods, the stillness adding a needed dimension of peace and tranquility to our tired, wondering minds. The thought of the solitude here on this special parcel of land at the very end of a road suited my Grizzly Adams mentality; and the proximity to Sandpoint would allow for Mike's need for civilization. It was the best of both of our worlds. The air was crisp, the day — everything — took on a mood of rightness. We drove back to the realtor's office. An offer was made, then the seller's counter-offer, a counter to the counter-offer, then acceptance.

We were going to move to Idaho!

Chapter 3

—Preparation For The Unknown—

I arrived in our new community during the last week of March 1987, having pulled a utility trailer — loaded with a solar hot water storage tank, three hot water solar panels, tools and stuff — behind my newly acquired 1983 four-wheel drive pick-up. However, spring break-up had arrived, preventing my pulling the trailer through the mud to the cabin, so I left it at Emma's and Mac's house, friends who just moved here — from Lake Almanor!

Emma had attended the last of the Ramtha sessions at our house, decided to move and had already bought a home and moved in prior to my arrival in the Sandpoint area. Right after we had purchased our land and had returned to Lake Almanor, Emma called to say that they had just returned from a trip.

"Where did you go?" I asked.

"A place called Sandpoint, Idaho —"

"Really?" I responded. "What did you do there?"

"Bought a house."

"That's interesting," I replied, "*we* just bought some property on *our* last trip"

"Where did you go?"

"A place called Sandpoint, Idaho."

It was a project. The cabin was added onto. I designed and helped build a house with a hot water and electrical system powered by the sun. Photovoltaic panels were installed on the roof, and a generator was put in place to charge the batteries during extended periods of gray skies. I purchased a used pump jack and a 12-volt motor, the kind of motor that motorizes wheelchairs, and installed it on the pump jack to pump water, in place of Bob's method of "keeping in shape." The whole project turned out — well, like it was *supposed* to.

Mike wisely stayed in California during the construction period. We had already built two other homes and our marriage had survived, but the third house? Besides, she understandably wanted her last summer on the lake, where she could bask in the sun, visit with her friends, and enjoy all that she would miss so much. In addition, the cabin would have been too small for both of us and our two-dog persons, but was just right for one, the one who was to work with the contractors and be on-site for any unexpected construction events.

During the period prior to actual construction, even though much time was devoted to the details of obtaining permits, dealing with contractors and laying out the position of the house on the land, I had many evenings to enjoy the land. I would walk through the woods that surrounded the cabin, looking at the trees, marveling at the different kinds of plants that chose to be a part of the web of life here in this corner of Idaho. Often, when I was apparently open — deeply appreciative of the sights and smells of the land — I would find a chill running through my body and a feeling of joy and oneness with Nature. And my eyes would fill with tears of happiness, not realizing that this feeling, this beautiful experience, was a sign that I was connecting with the Nature Spirits. But I did realize that I was happy, *really* happy.

As soon as I was settled, I knew it was time to explore the area, to see what existed outside of our land, to find what surprises lay in store just over the hill in the nearby meadows. Climbing into my truck and shifting into four-wheel drive, I ventured past the neighbor's cabin and up the small mountain to the northeast. The hill was steep and the rocks and spring mud made the going slow. It was apparent that no one had been on this road all winter. Driving to the top of the mountain, I stopped the truck, climbed out of the cab and found a fallen tree that would make a fine bench at the edge of the forest that could offer me a panoramic view of the area.

I sat there for some time, looking down on the Pend Oreille River as it meandered westward toward Washington.

A faint breeze brushed my cheeks, too faint to cause the pines above me to whisper. My eyes traced the slopes of the nearby hills covered with evergreens, the bright green patches of deciduous tamarack standing out, contrasting against the darker hues of the other trees not yet awakened to the call of spring.

I reflected on our new home, so different from the topography of Lake Almanor. But there was a resonance, a familiar feeling of peace and harmony in the company of the trees and grasses and spring flowers that were now appearing in the periphery of my vision. I sat there, preoccupied with the many things yet to do, not yet realizing that I was in the presence of intelligences I would soon feel and connect with on a very deep level.

On my return trip to the cabin, and as I passed the next door neighbor's property, a young woman, wearing a scarf on her head, blue jeans showing serious usage, and manure-sprinkled boots, came out of the barn, smiled and waved. As I stopped, she introduced herself as Dawn and told me that she and her husband Ray had been there for a few years, raised pigs, horses, chickens, taken in many stray or abandoned dogs and cats, and did gardening. She then offered me pig and horse manure for my planned vegetable garden.

The next morning, a large pick-up truck, stacked high with manure, and driven by this petite but apparently very strong young woman, was backed up to my garden location. Within minutes after we had unloaded the manure, her husband arrived, following behind a roto-tiller. My offer to do the roto-tilling was declined by Ray; He insisted he understood the temperament of the machine and would prefer to do it himself.

As he turned to my garden plot, and prior to starting the tiller, a look of concern crossed his face, concern, I soon learned, for the earthworms that would be chopped up. "This machine will cut up all those little guys," I remember him saying. In reflecting on that small event in the not too distant past, it is remarkable how my perception has changed. Now, I don't use any motorized means of turning the soil, not since Ray roto-tilled. Now, I am very careful not to damage any worm that arrives in the manure or exists in the soil. Now, I let flies out of the house, rather than killing them. Now, I capture yellow jackets and bees that arrive in our home by mistake, as well as the ubiquitous stink bugs, and return them to their natural habitat. Now, I allow the "weeds" to grow in the meadow and cut them only in the fall to reduce the fire potential. Now, I wouldn't think of using any chemical, even a biodegradable, benign one, to control pests or hasten the growth of the plants.

During late spring and summer, Dawn visited with me quite frequently, bringing with her questions, one of which I still remember to this day, and for good reason. At first, the questions related to family, where the children lived, what occupation I retired from, why we decided to move to Idaho (that one was not easy), then she dropped the bomb.

As I was walking toward the cabin with Dawn following me, the question "What's a multidimensional reality?" dropped into the conversation.

"What", I said, struggling to gather my defenses.

"What's a multidimensional reality?" Dawn repeated.

"Where did you hear that?"

"Do you know what it is?"

"I've heard of it. Where did you hear that expression?" I said, trying to divert her attention long enough to further prepare myself, to formulate a plausible, acceptable answer.

This woman, Dawn, my neighbor, didn't know anything about me, except that I was retired from real estate, came from California, had two sons, and that my wife was in Lake Almanor. How could she — why *would* she — ask me a metaphysical question like this? It was mind-boggling.

I don't remember exactly how I explained to Dawn what a multidimensional reality is, but I know that I was sufficiently vague, purposefully so, to avoid a discussion about metaphysics at this early time in our neighborly relationship. But in the conversation that followed, Dawn explained to me that she was convinced she was going insane. She was hearing things, phrases that were totally foreign to her; someone was talking in her head. She explained that she saw what she termed "glow balls," not just at night, while asleep, but in the middle of the day, and that, in some manner, she was being transported to "places" that were completely unfamiliar to her. She *knew* she was losing it.

This was a delicate situation. How could I — in a rational manner — explain to this lady that she was probably being contacted by entities in another reality? How could I approach this subject, introduce the concept of "channeling" without offering her reinforcement that she was, indeed, insane ?

I really don't know what I did to convince her that she was not insane, but I remember it was not easy. Evening after evening we talked — she, explaining her "craziness," me, offering alternatives. Maybe it was my knowing that she was *not* insane that convinced her, maybe it was the sign that I made with a marker pen on a cardboard boxtop that I would hold up every time she claimed insanity during our conversations, which said, "Dawn — you are *not* crazy." Maybe it was because, deep down, she knew she was okay.

In one of our conversations, I remember explaining that she shouldn't be surprised that she might verbalize the thoughts that came into her head; and they would not be at all like her usual thought patterns; and, in fact, the voice might not even sound like her own. She quickly explained that it had already happened, and that Ray had recorded it. Then I explained that a similar experience had jolted Jane Roberts — that she had what appeared to be a "rush" of information, that her reaction was in many ways similar to Dawn's. This bit of information seemed to help.

"At least," I could hear her say to herself, "someone else has been involved in this phenomenon and hasn't been committed." Hope seemed to gradually enter her thought processes, but a midnight visit, a surprise visit, was not exactly expected by either Dawn or myself.

The cabin was perfect for me during the construction period of the house. The main floor was about about 15 feet by 18 feet, including the kitchen and the sitting area. As one entered the cabin, the kitchen sink was on the left and a large woodstove rested on a raised, brick hearth opposite the sink. On the right was a very steep stairway led to the loft — the bedroom — which consisted of an area large enough to accommodate a bed and a small, three-drawer chest.

To have room to enter the bed on the right, the left side of the bed was pushed up against one of the two windows, which made it convenient for scanning the southern star-filled sky, for seeing the deer feed in the light of the moon and bedding down on the edge of the woods, to see the light mist that drifted over the garden just before sun-up, to hear the crack of a limb as a large mammal moved through the forest.

The window next to my bed was always left open, except during a hard rain, allowing the fresh breezes to flow into the loft. The air was clear and refreshing, and I remember being really tired at the end of this particular day. Summer daylight lasts longer here above the 48th parallel, the outline of the trees in the forest being visible until 10:00 p.m. or so. It wasn't unusual for me to go to bed before it was completely dark.

When I was awakened, the night was moonless, causing the woods, the woodshed and the garden to blend into the blackness with no definition, no separation. I don't remember ever seeing a blacker night. Peering into the unfathomable night was like part of a deep dream, a dream that included the impenetrable blackness and a knock at the door. A knock at the door? Who? Why?

Still half asleep, I rolled onto my right side and muttered into the abysmal night, "Who is it?"

A voice came back from the darkness, a voice I didn't immediately recognize. "It's Dawn. May I come in?"

The voice sounded hollow, without emotion, without anxiety, detached. "Just a minute, until I put on some clothes."

There was no response from the cabin steps..

As I opened the door, Dawn walked past me, apparently in an unseeing state, sat on the elevated hearth next to the woodstove and spoke. The body was hers, the vocal chords that produced the sounds were hers, but the voice was not her own. The voice explained that it was group mind Lumar, that Dawn was a part of their group, that they were calling on me for help to aid in the process of integration. They remained in her body for probably five or ten minutes, speaking to me, calling me by another name, a name of a being that they knew me to be, a being of which I later learned I am a part. At that time, never having witnessed a multidimensional transition, not knowing that I was a part of another entity in other dimensions, not being entirely awake or aware, was like dreamsville continued.

I told the Lumar group I would be glad to help in any way I could, but I didn't know what I could do to facilitate this process, didn't know what they needed from me, didn't know what to do next, having had no experience with this sort of thing. They obviously had a lot more confidence in my abilities than I did.

"Just believe in the instrument (Dawn) and in us."

They left her body.

Somehow I had presence of mind enough to record this first visit. Evidently, the Lumar group made a note of how I seemed to be fond of recording.

Dawn's body shook violently as they departed, as if she was experiencing a seizure. Unaccustomed to their vibration, and group mind Lumar being unaccustomed to a later-refined method of arriving and departing, the seizure caused Dawn to fall against the woodstove from her sitting position, thumping her head against the unyielding cold steel. Feeling inadequate and totally unprepared for this midnight experience, but wanting to offer her aid, I stood, crossed the room and reached out for her as she returned to this reality. She withdrew, frightened, insisted she was all right, and headed for the door.

"You'd better borrow my flashlight," I said. "It's really dark out there — no moon."

"I got over here, so I can sure get home," the dazed voice, this time Dawn's, replied.

Less than five feet into the darkness past the cabin steps, a bewildered Dawn returned, and asked to borrow my flashlight, not understanding how she got to my cabin; in fact, she didn't remember coming over.

The house I had designed was to use sun to provide electricity that would power the house, but since all that was in place at that time was a couple of solar panels and two batteries, the thought of a refrigerator, at this state, wasn't even considered. My perishables were stored in a small cooler on the north side of the cabin. The cooler was buried in the earth almost to the lid to improve its limited insulation. It became obvious that the Lumar beings and/or Dawn had knowledge of my morning habit of going to the cooler to retrieve juice or whatever could be found.

The morning following the night-time visit, I made my morning trip to the cooler, preoccupied with the events of the night before, and found a cassette tape on the lid. That particular morning, curiosity even over-rode my desire for the first cup of coffee, so re-entering the cabin, cassette in hand, I sat down on the couch, popped the tape into my machine, and listened to this short, but very interesting recording:

> "Entity, you seem to take great stock in so transcribing, therefore, this is yours.

> "The transition is complete. We thank you, entity consciousness. Your belief in her/our reality coalesced the reality of completeness into the third plane reality.

> "We regret the intrusion into your selected unconsciousness to yourself.

> "It shall take small practice for our completeness to entertain the ways of this planal existence comfortably. We shall make small, hopefully unnoticeable mistakes for a time, but the third plane personality of our being understands the movements that are correct within this existence, for comfortable acceptance of this, the third plane, earth.

> "The third plane self of our being thanks you for your time and patience. We, the entire, thank you for the aid you projected."

When I spoke to Dawn later that day and thanked her for the tape, her recollection of bringing it over was vague, like in a dream, and she had no knowledge whatsoever of making the recording. She was also surprised when I asked her if she had ever studied and acted as a Shakespearean performer, the reason for my question being, the enunciation, the timing, the breathing were so *perfect* on the tape. She said she had no training or experience in the theater.

I pondered over the one statement on the tape: "We regret the intrusion into your selected unconsciousness to yourself." I later learned that the person that group mind Lumar saw living in the cabin as a neighbor of Dawn's was not third planal Orin, but was, in fact, what I would term a being on another plane, a portion of which I identify as myself, Orin, here and now. They didn't know, in our first contact that I, as a human, had a limited view of my totality, so they assumed that I had consciously chosen to remain ignorant of the other aspects of myself.

Dawn quickly adapted to her new cosmic friends, but for a time resisted their desire to speak through her, still somewhat convinced in the recesses of her mind that she wasn't balanced. She felt that she had little control over their arrival, and their lack of understanding as to the right time, right place, did provide her with some understandable anxiety.

On more than one occasion, *group* was held back by Dawn when they tried to speak to strangers. I was witness to one instance of this indiscretion when Dawn, Ray and I went to dinner and group almost insisted on talking to a lady who stopped by our table. Dawn's face turned beet red as she strained to hold back the words, phrases and philosophical discussions that were trying to find their verbal outlet through "the instrument."

As time passed, Dawn's group became more comfortable, more adept at expressing themselves. They gradually learned that it was not in third planal good taste to surprise friends and strangers with a new voice, thoughts and attitudes emanating from the mouth of Dawn. But since I was a kind of charter member, they felt free to discuss many topics. The discussions took place mostly in the evening, on the cabin steps.

We — group, Dawn and I — spent many hours together in early summer of 1987. They explained to me that there were many of them here, responding to the call from Gaia, our earth. They told me that there were many cells (my terminology) in the group, each with seven entities, and that each entity was involved in the process of transceiving — receiving and projecting energies of harmony for the benefit of earth. I learned from Dawn that she spent two to three hours in the very early morning of each day picking up vibrations from the entire group and redirecting them through and around our planet.

The profound, sometimes very abstract conversations became a lot for my 3 P mind to absorb. For awhile it became almost too much, since I had no sustained contact with other humans during this period, and I lived in a constant learning, analyzing mode. The one exception was the other neighbor, Rich, who arrived on his dirt bike one day and said "How about coming to our house for spaghetti tonight?"

Back to this reality, I thought.

During this mentally stretching, expanding, challenging period in a new environment, it didn't occur to me that it was unusual, incredibly unusual, for one to move into a new state, and to find that the only two, full-time neighbors we had would be a part of the cosmic puzzle. In fact, I neither saw the puzzle, nor understood that we were a part of it.

In late October 1987, after the house was mostly completed, I drove to California to assist in the big move. After the hired mover had loaded his van, and my pickup and utility trailer were weighed down with all they could handle, Mike got behind the wheel of her Honda, accompanied by two excited dog passengers, and the caravan headed north.

When we arrived in Idaho, and the furniture and endless stacks of boxes were unloaded in the house, Mike went to work finishing the cabinets in her meticulous manner, and in spite of the ongoing search though cartons for the right cookware, she somehow was able to find time to do incredible culinary tricks on a two-burner camp stove. Shortly thereafter, I plumbed the main house for liquid petroleum gas, we bought a propane cookstove and were more or less settled in for the winter.

Prior to designing our house, I first checked out the national weather services solar map which indicated we would have about 20 percent less sun than where we lived in California. That would still be plenty, I thought. I didn't realize that the map I looked at really dealt with *average* annual solar hours, and since our summer daylight in north Idaho stretches from 4:00 a.m. to 10:00 p.m., the cumulative light hours adds up to lots of *summer* sun, but not much winter sun. We were in for some surprises.

The first winter was — as I now refer to it — a learning experience. The woodstove, even though large, was no match for the cold that drifted in — no, was *sucked* in — from the "sun space," which I had designed to store heat in the winter from the expected solar gain. It became a "*cold* space," until we installed a sliding glass door between the sun space and the main part of the house, then added insulated drapes. The connecting hoses to the circulating hot water pump in the attic developed a leak, allowing the hot water to cascade down the kitchen drywall and get under the linoleum, causing it to buckle. The well pump kept freezing up until some of the connections were changed or removed, but in spite of these and other conveniently forgotten events, we survived the first winter quite well. As the signs of spring showed us the hope of sun-filled days, we emerged as fully mobile beings from our chrysalis case, renewed, awaiting the next movement within us.

During the first winter, Mike had the opportunity to meet our other full time neighbors, located about one-half mile from our house, the ones who had invited me over for spaghetti. Rich and Mary, though not "metaphysical," in the generally accepted sense, were, and are, on an awakening path, though they may not feel inclined to embrace that choice of words.

When Mike first met Rich, he had a .357 Magnum strapped on his hip, was carrying a beer, and talked of hunting. Since then, the .357 has disappeared, the hunting trips have been forgotten, and these interests have been replaced by his becoming the areas most dedicated protector of wildlife, including his determination to win the lottery and purchase many parcels of land to the north of us and convert it to a wildlife sanctuary.

So Mike, in the winter of 1987, met our only real neighbors: Dawn and Ray, who lived closest, and Rich and Mary, on the "other road." Dawn, who "just happened" to undergo a transition that allowed her access to the multidimensional realities she had asked me about shortly after our first meeting, and Rich and Mary, undergoing transformation. How *interesting!*

My wife had told me for many years (did it happen on the day of our marriage?) that I should stop and learn to appreciate the little things in life, and this sounded like a marvelous thing to do — some day. But after our move to Idaho and my success in separating myself both physically and mentally from the business world, I was left with no excuses *not* to experience the small wonders of life. The urgings of my wife and now my inner voice became a stereo concert, playing the theme, "Stop and smell the flowers." But then there was the solo part with the little voice within singing a new song. "Yes," the little voice said. "You're really supposed to smell the flowers, to pay attention to the little things in life — and buy a camera." I'm supposed to buy a camera?

We had a small camera that took pretty good pictures, but our use of it was so limited that each time we prepared to take a snapshot we had to review the operating manual to see how it was done. My decision to buy a better camera involved an outlay of cash that was fairly substantial, and being convinced that our small Idaho town would not have what I wanted at an acceptable price, I said to myself, "I'll just go into town and shop, then I'll go to Spokane and buy one at a discount store."

Eay, Dawn's invisible spokesperson from group, once described a "coincidence" as a "cooperative incident." How fitting that definition was during this camera episode, and since these "incidents" were becoming quite commonplace in our lives, I shouldn't have been surprised to learn that the camera store had just what I needed: a used camera and all the accessories at a substantial savings.

I purchased the camera, lenses, carrying case, plus a couple of rolls of film, and went home to take pictures of wildflowers and the beautiful, so-called "weeds" on our property.

I learned how to load the film in the camera, and remembering what the camera store owner told me, I set the shutter speed and stepped into the meadow area to the south of our house. It was now July 1988, and the prolific wildflowers, many of which are referred to by the agricultural community as "weeds," were at the apex of their beauty. The colors were overwhelming. The purples of the clover blending with the orange hock, the white and yellow daisies. No wonder I was supposed to take a more intimate look at Nature's miracles! Just kneeling or sitting on the ground, getting closer to these wonders, seeing some of the intricacies that Nature has created in the leaves and blossoms was, by itself, an altering experience. I had purchased some diopters for close-up work, and looking through the lens was like looking at a whole new world, a world I had never known or seen. Occasionally a chill would run through my body, just as it had when I walked the land prior to starting construction of our home. I began mentally talking to these wondrous creatures, telling them how beautiful they were, how I would care for them, how I appreciated their being where they were. I started to take pictures with my camera — *never realizing...*

Chapter 4

—Photo Magic—

During the spring and summer of 1988, Gayl Kellenberger, who lives in Montana, was offering channeling workshops. Mike and I both enjoyed Gayl's sense of humor, her vibrant personality, her sharing philosophy, and admired her clarity as a channel. The first workshop of Gayl's we attended was held at Peggy Fogarty's house, a few miles north of town. This was about a week before the very memorable one at the Unity Church in Sandpoint.

The workshop at the church had to do with working with the Devic Kingdom, which was completely new to me, not having heard the word Deva, before. During the workshop, I learned that word Deva — pronounced day-va or dee-va — is a Sanskrit word meaning "shining one," or "Being of Light," and sometimes interpreted as "Angel." During the break on the first day of the weekend event, Gayl was showing and explaining to some of us the interesting things she carried with her when she did workshops, how she came into possession of a particular crystal, a pendant and a photo of a flower with a blue aura around it. The photograph intrigued me. I had never seen one quite like it.

"What's the blue light?" I asked Gayl.

"That's a Deva," she explained. "That picture was taken by Vicki Smith from Oregon."

I asked for Vicki's mailing address, explaining that I had just purchased a camera for the purpose of taking pictures of wildflowers and other nature photos.

"Bring your camera to the workshop tomorrow morning and I'll ask the class to give it special energy," Gayl said.

In retrospect, it seems clear she was being guided.

I have often marveled at how people arrive in our lives —

sometimes for just a moment — to provide the needed boost, suggest a book, recommend a place to go, say a word that resonates deep within us and allows us to know that a new road is open for our travel, for our exploration. This was happening more and more in our lives: the meeting with a piano tuner who cautiously suggested we might want to join the small group at Lake Almanor; the books, like *Seth Speaks* which were "accidentally" introduced into our lives; the meeting of the stranger in the Mount Shasta bookstore who suggested another Ramtha book; the owner of the bookstore renting us some Ramtha videos; on and on it goes — synchronicity becoming a part of our lives; and this "chance" meeting with Gayl, which now I know wasn't chance at all; it was to be the beginning of an exciting adventure in alternate realities.

Before we had even heard about Gayl in the spring of 1988, I was visiting with Kelly, one of the employees in a local bookstore. During our conversation, Kelly mentioned that there would be a channeling by Gayl taking place at Peggy Fogarty's during the forthcoming weekend for the "old timers." We were far from being old timers, if that meant we had lived here for a long time, or had gone to Gayl's workshops before, but I called Peggy. "Hi, Peggy, this is Orin Bridges"

"Who?"

"Orin Bridges. I just learned of the channeling by Gayl to be held at your house."

"Uh, well, I'm not sure there is any room at this late date. Where did you hear about it?"

"At Booktrader II."

Peggy then asked a series of questions concerning our background in metaphysics, where were we were from, how long had we lived in the Sandpoint area, were we acquainted with Gayl. This was becoming quite an interview. I persisted, giving Peggy the answers she evidently needed.

Later I learned that she was "screening" people who attended for the first time, since they had had an incident in which a person became frightened when Gayl channeled another voice/entity.

Peggy cautiously asked if we had experienced channeling, and when I assured her we had on many occasions, the interview was over, and we were welcomed to the gathering.

It was unlike me to call a stranger and ask to be invited to a "closed" meeting; it was unlike me to persist in trying to obtain an invitation to a gathering where we might not be welcome, to even make that kind of effort to see and hear a channel I had never heard of before. Obviously, this was a very important event, one that we should attend — unlikely or not.

The workshop was more than we expected. The channeled information was timely, the collective energies of all those who attended was positive and loving, the day was enjoyable plus.

On the second day of Gayl's workshop at the Unity Church building, I brought my camera, as she had suggested. Gayl took the camera and sat on her stool, the one prop she always carried with her. The stool was Gayl's speaking platform, the place she sat when speaking to her audiences, her "grounding" vehicle. When the unseen entities arrived in Gayl's body, they seldom remained seated, however, preferring to roam back and forth in front of the audience, often gesturing, often joking with the audience. Before the channeling began this particular Sunday morning, Gayl made an announcement I shall never forget.

I can still see Gayl perched on her stool, my camera cradled in her arms, and as the gathering became quiet and attentive, she looked out over the group gathered in the room, some cross-legged on the floor, some sitting on chairs, some standing, and made this announcement: "Orin has purchased this camera in order to take pictures of Devas."

I didn't want to interrupt her, but I didn't say that. I told her I bought the camera to take pictures of wildflowers and other nature photos. The statement — intentional, accidental, channeled, intuitive or all of the above — was prophetic. The camera was passed from person to person as planned, and everyone held it.

Some of the attendees looked through the camera, some closed their eyes and allowed their loving energy to flow in and through it, some blessed it. There was hardly a person there that didn't know more about the camera than I did. But my lack of knowledge about photography, I discovered, was a very important lack. Had I been knowledgeable, I would have known that what showed up on my first roll of film would have to be related to mechanical problems, but since I was without technical knowledge, I was completely unsure, which turned out to be an advantage.

One of the persons who we met at Gayl's event, a man with some photographic knowledge, a man named Michael, approached me during the break Sunday morning and asked if he could come to our house to meditate. Unusual, my logical mind was saying, that this person, whom we just met, would want to visit with us and meditate. Unusual it was, in more ways than one.

I drew a map so Michael could find our house, we set a time and date for his arrival, and dismissed this unusual event as we turned our interest back to the workshop.

During the next few days following Gayl's workshop, I spent some more time in our meadow, photographing wild-flowers and beautiful weeds. When I took exposure number 24, I rewound the film, opened the back of the camera, like the instruction book said, and removed the exposed film. It would be developed by the camera store, and the prints would be back Tuesday.

When I picked up the processed film on Tuesday morning, I anxiously opened the package of prints on the way home to see how I did. The wild flowers showed up pretty good, but in three of the 24 exposures, there were some lights and shapes on the prints that I couldn't, as a novice, under-stand. My tentative conclusion was that the lights were caused by some mistake I had made in my first serious attempt at photography or that there was a problem with the camera.

Another "cooperative incident" happened when Michael arrived. The sliding glass door was open, the warm summer breezes were moving gently across our meadow, floating through the open doorway into the living room where the prints were spread out on the coffee table. In retrospect (I seem to say that a lot now), it was interesting that he had never been to our home before, this Michael person, and that he had chosen to arrive on that particular day, the day when the prints were laid out on the coffee table. "Isn't this a little odd?" I might have asked myself. But there was no noticeable hint at this stage of awareness that synchronicity was already taking place.

Michael had a working knowledge of photography, which was evident when he asked questions of me at Gayl's workshop regarding the kind of lens I had on the camera and other things I didn't know. So, when he saw the prints on the coffee table and asked about the strange lights in the photographs, I felt it was a regular photographer-type question.

"Probably something I did, or didn't do, since I don't know photography — or maybe it's a light leak in the camera," I said.

Michael studied the prints more closely. "Looks more like a Light *Being* to me."

"A what?"

At Michael's request, I led him to the spot in the meadow where I had taken one of the photos. Crouching down, touching the earth with one knee and then one hand, he began nodding his head. In agreement? With what? After a few moments he stood up and commented that there was definitely a being in the vicinity, and he would call it a meadow Deva.

The original cabin on the land was left as part of our house, separated by the sun space and garage, remote enough from the main house to provide a quiet and private location for guests, with its small but okay kitchen and bathroom. The cabin is where the man, Michael, and I went to meditate after his "contact" with the intelligence in the meadow. In a sort of guided meditation, he suggested I mentally ask for the name of the being.

I received the name, "Andrea." Being very unsure of my impressions, I hesitated to say her name, believing I might be making it up. I wasn't making it up. *Andrea* was the Light Being that showed up on my first roll of film.

My first inclination (being of sound and logical mind, of course) was to seek validation that these images were really "Beings of Light." I went to the camera store where I had

"Andrea." The form you see is the closest to humanoid of any energy formations I have recorded. I sense she projected this form to get my attention, since she was the first Devic energy to appear on my film.

purchased the camera, the store that had sent the negatives out for developing. I learned that the three ladies that worked there were all photographers, two of them having had their work displayed locally, all three active in the Sandpoint Camera Club, and one now a free-lance professional. They would *certainly* have the answers if it related to something more practical than a Being of Light. After much conversation as to what these lights really were, all three agreed on what they were not...

"Does it look like a light leak to you?" asked one lady of another.

"Not really. Besides, the frames that are affected are not sequential. They are in various locations on the roll."

"Lens flare?"

"He's shooting *away* from the sun."

"Heat?"

"No."

"Are you saying you don't know what they are?" I asked

hopefully.

"Right — we don't know."

A couple of months later, all three ladies were curious enough to ask what the images were. I told them, then I loaned them my Findhorn Garden Book.

Each roll, it seemed, would have something in the batch that was "unusual." Some of the light images would have been overlooked, except for Eay of the group mind Lumar, who suggested we look at other prints, ones that I had put away and considered unimportant.

One roll was processed by a one-hour lab, and the poor lady who ran it through the machine explained to me in great detail how there could not be any light inside the machine that developed the film and processed it; so, that eliminated the developing process as a potential source of light. She, too, was unable to explain what or why. I was rapidly coming to the end of this logical trip I was on. I had a gift; it was now quite clear. But why me? Why would I be able to take pictures of non-physical entities, and what would I do with them?

It wasn't long after that when I found I could, on occasion, pick up Andrea's thought impressions in meditation. At first, I would sit and feel I was "making up" some of the thoughts that entered my mind. But it was a nice game, this make believe, and some of the thoughts were, well, not exactly things I might say. I verbalized these thoughts and put them on tape. At first, the words seemed like they were five minutes apart, and the playback took me forever just to hear what I had said. Since I didn't want to open my eyes to push "record" and "stop," the next best thing was for me to rig up a remote cord with a push button on the end of it that would activate the "pause" function.

When I felt the surging, the lifting movement of energy within me, I would push the button and the recorder would record. When I released it, the cassette would stop, but would remain in the record mode. This cut out all of the pauses — and there were plenty of them — between thoughts and words. Soon, I was able to hear Andrea's "voice" in my head. I "imagined" how she might sound. What a loving, gentle entity.

Was I really receiving her thought transmissions? Could these thoughts, which came in the form of impressions, possibly be my own from another aspect of the Orin personality? Were these "conversations" a means of releasing an inner longing to be in another reality? Could I, would I, ever see her in form? Did she *have* form? Was she *real?* It wasn't until much later that I was really convinced that I was connecting with Andrea. After an experience I was privileged to share with some other people, there was no doubt. This experience convinced me that Andrea *was* and *is* real.

A year and a half passed, and I was totally unprepared for the emotional impact of hearing Andrea's voice through another person. I had never heard her speak, audibly, but at the same time, I could identify her gentle energy and loving thoughts, and I felt closely connected with the Devic Kingdom that this Being represented. I spent more and more time in the garden, in the woods and in our meadow, connecting with the Nature Spirits and the garden Deva, Angelica. (Yes, I received her name in meditation, also.) When I walked in the meadow, I tried to avoid walking on some of the more beautiful flower-weeds, but as I came closer to understanding that everything was beautiful, whether it was a blade of grass or orange hock weed, I realized it would be very difficult to avoid walking on *everything* beautiful, including the ground, although there were times that I felt like it was entirely possible.

Starting in November 1989, we had meetings at our house relating to a concept referred to as "double bonding." The teachings dealt with the interaction of humans with one another and with all other species. The guidelines were simple: Each species has a right to exist, each species has a right of self-determination, each species has a right of non-interference by others. *Double bonding* means a bonding with those of like beliefs and the bonding of love with those of opposing beliefs. In lieu of the tendency to convert opposing-belief people to our own set of beliefs, the premise was to allow them to be themselves, and to celebrate the differences that make us unique.

We were a small group that joined together every couple

of weeks. One of the regular attendees was, understandably, our neighbor Dawn.

By this time, Dawn had become a very clear channel, and as she and I hiked the nearby hills and meadows on a fairly regular basis, I was introduced to a grand array of multidimensional, or other dimensional, beings. She was my guide into Nature's invisible realms, helping me to become more and more in tune with the Devic Kingdom, translating impressions from the energies in Nature into linear words. During this period, my senses seemed to come more alive, I was able to verbalize some of the information that I picked up, Dawn encouraging me to "allow," as we communicated with these various entities.

I am still in awe of the circumstances that led us to this land where our neighbor needed help in making a very important transition and then to find that she became my communication link to the Nature intelligences.

On one occasion we were walking near the top of the mountain that overlooks our properties, and we both paused, looking into a heavily shaded area of the woods where many trees had fallen. A raven was calling from one of the treetops, and the energies that were drawing us were unmistakable. Dawn started toward the densest part of the woods.

I hesitated. "Dawn, I don't think we should enter. I sense it is a Deva sanctuary"

"The guardian of the sanctuary, the raven, says it's okay to enter, for they know we mean no harm," she assured me.

So, we entered.

In the low light of the shaded woods with my camera set for automatic shutter speed, I took two photographs. Neither photo should have come out. The light was very limited and the automatic mode meant the shutter would stay open until it had enough light to close. Plus, the camera was hand-held, and with slow shutter speed there would be no way to avoid camera shake.

Incredibly, the photos came out — greatly under-exposed — but no camera shake was noticeable, a phenomenon that defies a logical explanation. One of the photos includes a very strong white and pink light, formed like a

"Deva Sanctuary." Although I was reluctant to enter their domain, the Devic energies projected this formation onto a greatly under-exposed frame.

shaft, in the middle of the dark forest.

As time went on, my wife Mike, and I spent long hours conversing with Dawn, as well as with other entities that transmitted through Dawn. Eay, our main contact with group mind Lumar, was always helpful and informative, explaining their philosophy, how their belief did not include good and bad, right and wrong, or any of the dualities that we perceive exist here on this plane. "All is well," was Eay's most common response to any of our planetary, national or personal crises.

During this same period of time, Mike was beginning to "see" images of beings in our home and on our land. On one late summer day in 1988, I was out in the garden with my camera (Why would I take my camera to the garden?), and Mike spoke from the sliding glass door that opens onto our deck: "There's somebody behind you."

I turned and saw nothing.

Dawn then stepped to the door, and directing my attention to one of the potato plants that was in full bloom, suggested I take a picture. I did, and a white funnel of energy clearly showed in the finished print.

On a very memorable Thursday evening during the summer of 1989, the double-bonding meeting concluded and there were just five of us remaining in our living room, sitting on the floor. It wasn't unusual for an entity to arrive via Dawn's body, but this evening I was in for an experience that was totally unexpected.

Dawn indicated there was someone who wanted to talk to me, closed her eyes and easily slipped into a trance state. As the consciousness of this being entered her body, and before it identified itself, I knew who it was. The softness, gentleness, compassion, the feeling of unconditional love which was projected in the room and into our small group was exactly as I had heard and experienced for over a year in meditation. It was Andrea! The emotional impact was almost too much to bear. I greeted her through tears that filled my eyes, then washed down my cheeks, tears from the heart, from a deep remembrance long buried within my cellular memory.

My emotions were so charged I can still recall this first "meeting" as if it were yesterday. One of her first comments was "I am always with you, Orin," the same phrase I always hear when my intent is to connect with her. She then explained that verbal communication is not her preference and, in fact, is not needed, since we are in constant communication. I knew it — but I didn't know it. I now know that she is constantly with me in all my photographic endeavors, this beautiful being, this queen of the Devic Kingdom.

This was Andrea's first attempt to speak through a human and was unable to open Dawn's eyes. She asked me to move closer to her, and she touched my face, braille-like, brushing away some of my tears, connecting now in a physical manner, tracing my countenance with her forefinger, experiencing the sensation of touch. It was a lifting, joy-filled experience, one I shall remember...forever.

As time went on, I realized that there seemed to be certain circumstances that allowed me to obtain these unusual photographs, but my first realization that I couldn't "make it happen" came when I went to Montana to visit with

"Andrea — another view." The vortex shape appears frequently.

Carol and Arne Hovin.

The Hovins were building a new home on some very special land, were working and communicating with the Devas in the layout of their garden, and after being shown some of my early photographs by Gayl — the same Gayl who held the channeling workshops in Sandpoint and elsewhere — it seemed quite natural that they would want to capture the Nature intelligences on film.

Soon after the Hovins contacted me, I went to Montana to meet this marvelous couple. After being extended a warm greeting, followed by an enthusiastic tour of their beautiful new home, they guided me to their garden, explained that they would leave me alone with the Devas so I would be uninterrupted in my work, and went about their chores.

As soon as I entered the garden area, I felt the strong vibrations they had spoken of, powerful and loving. It was clear to me that this garden was alive in both a physical and etheric sense. There was no question about it. I was going to photograph many of these Devic energies, here at Hovin's Clarstar Farms.

I attached my camera to my tripod and connected the cable release so I could trigger the shutter with little effort. I sat on the ground next to a beautiful, large crystal, the centerpiece of their garden, and allowed myself to move gently out of my active state into one of peace and unity with the surroundings. The immersion into this reality was immediate and complete, and as I sensed the Beings of Nature that were present, they seemed to reach out, their vibrations gentle, soft, welcoming me into their unseen reality. How wonderful, I thought, that the Hovins were so aware of working with these loving entities.

This was my first "assignment," my first attempt to do any Deva photography out of our immediate area, not knowing what to expect. Did Andrea or other Devas travel with me? Were they alerted to my travels and made aware of my location? Were some locations better than others for this phenomenon to take place? These questions and many more flitted in and out of my conscious mind like hummingbirds, here for a moment, then out of sight in a flash.

Many of the answers to these questions have since come to me through various, most often, unexpected sources; a person's comments, a magnet-like attraction to a book in which another part of the puzzle appears, a feeling that I have known it all along. Other answers remain obscure, retained in a sort of cosmic time-release capsule, preparing for their infusion into my brain at the precise moment when other interactive data are in place.

In September 1990, I received information that, in many ways, validated my feelings about taking pictures of the multidimensional beings, especially the Devic energies, and clearly demonstrates how our intentions and experiences are a part of our vibrational field. It came about after a wonderfully emotional day in the woods.

After school starts and the summer vacations are completed, the woods become more quiet, and in some areas one can walk miles without seeing or hearing a human. This particular fall day I was sure no one was within five miles of my hiking trail in northern Idaho, above upper Priest Lake, almost to Canada. The vacationers had deserted the woods, the forest was left to the animals and the few fortunates like myself; but I wasn't alone.

The trail I was following traveled through an old growth of Douglas fir trees. On my right as I walked, these magnificent giants stretched to the sky, growing from a steep slope above me, making them appear even taller. On my left, the mountain dropped off sharply, permitting me a bird's eye view of these wonderful old trees. Advancing at a slow pace, I felt the trees' energies moving, pouring out toward me, encompassing me like an invisible mother's arms. I continued to walk, and as I did, all the emotions I wanted to express to these beautiful beings poured forth, verbally and in the unspoken words of the heart.

I told the trees I didn't know why I was to come to this magical place, but now it was clear that I had to connect with them, and in so doing, enter this state of rapture, their beauteous forms and vibrational emanations expressing what words cannot. Tears filled my eyes and I let myself cry, joyfully unashamed of this great outpouring of love as it overtook me. The experience was one of release, and a kind of remembrance of ancient times.

Later that day, as I drove toward home, but still in the upper Priest River Falls area, I stopped my truck, got out to walk through and admire a grove of Red Cedars, pausing long enough to take one picture, a picture that, when developed, showed a vibrant blue energy extending from the top of the cedars and seemingly entering the earth. I knew it was a "thank you" from the trees for recognizing their consciousness...Thank you, trees.

I sent a print of this picture to our friends, Pamela Chase and Jonathan Pawlick, for they had just completed their third book, this one titled, *Trees for Healing* (Newcastle Publishing). Shortly after sending the photo, I received a letter from them, thoughtfully enclosing this very appropriate and timely information channeled by Jonathan:

"I am the overlighting Deva for planet earth. you have asked me to share an understanding of the process

"Red Cedar Trees." A "Thank You" for recognizing their conciousness.

of manifestation of life-force energy as it is related to the kingdoms of Nature. To begin, let me first state that each life species in Nature has the capacity to project the purity of its essence out from itself. The light that you see is a composite energy of the species that are present in that given area. The reason that this is so, is that the manifestation of that energy by any one individual species would indeed create an excessive drain on the life force energy of that species...

"You can sense any life force energy in Nature when your intentions are pure and you emanate unconditional love from your heart. Species of Nature do not instantaneously open themselves to interact with the human kingdom. In many instances you must prove through continued loving actions that your intentions are truly pure.

"Before you enter the physical space of a species,

your intention has indeed preceded the physical encounter. Interaction with the human kingdom is not limited by space or time. For example, when you are kind to the plants in your immediate space, that kindness is felt outside your immediate area. When you enter the environment of other plants, they are already familiar with the energy patterns of your actions.

"Many lifestreams believe that their energies do not extend out beyond the physical vehicle, and that the physical vehicle is self-contained. The message of the photograph is that you interact with others even when you do not have direct physical contact with them. The patterns that emerge from within you are being received by other lifestreams, including the kingdoms of Nature.

"The light pattern that you see in the photograph is symbolic of the infinite nature of what you know as energy. It is a statement that everything is ongoing, and that death is merely another step in the growth process. You see, when you change your focus to reflect a more cosmic way of being, then your relationship to self and to all other forms of life becomes more positive and pure.

"Look around you. Get to know the infinite variety of life species that is part of our space. When you enter this sacred trust with Nature, all that you do will have healing, harmony and balance as the corner-stone of life itself.

"There is much compassion and empathy within the being who takes these photographs. Because he is living harmoniously with his environment, species in Nature will continue to open themselves to him. The process itself must continue to be an effortless one, for truly the energy emanations take place when there is flow within his being.

"You are all lights that are bringing illumination and an elevation in consciousness for the human kingdom. Be at peace and know that we are ever present with you, that we truly support the spiritual service that you are undertaking. In oneness, I am with thee"

Since the visit to Hovin's Clarstar Farms in Montana was my first "assignment," the results were very educational. After shooting 60 frames, and feeling the energies so strongly, I was surprised that I was was receiving a strong impression that perhaps no energy formations would appear, but not to be concerned. *Don't be concerned?*

As soon as I finished taking the pictures, I went directly to a local photo lab to have the prints developed, wishing to leave the Hovins with a set of prints of these Beings of Light. The educational part of this experience showed me — quite clearly — that "sensing" the energies doesn't mean they will show up on film. "Wanting" them to show up negates the process, since it puts effort in the way of joyful expression. This first assignment taught me that there is much more to this process than taking pictures. The "process," if you can call it that, involves being open, being one with Nature, but with no expectations.

What showed up on film was a collection of good prints — good color, good composition, good contrast, good exposure — but no "beings," except one small, flame-shaped formation appearing in a random photo I took looking south across their land, not in their beautiful, energy-inhabited garden.

When I went to pick up the finished prints, the owner of the photo lab said there would be a slight delay, since one of the prints showed a magenta sky. He explained that he was well acquainted with the film I was using and it did not lean toward magenta. He had run the film through his machine three times with different filters, but try as he did, the off-colored sky would not change. I assured him it was not a problem, thinking to myself that everything in Nature is vibratory, color included, allowing for the possibility that energies could show up as a color, rather than a shape.

A person living in the proximity of the Hovins has since channeled the Devic energy of Clarstar Farms, communicating with the being that showed itself as the color magenta. The Montana experience was the beginning of other color experiences. In addition to Montana magenta, I also had the same color show up in Colorado. Sepia tones dominated some photos I took in the woods and by the river near our home, and since my logical mind wanted a piece of the action, I allowed it to participate — in a deductive reasoning sort of way — hoping to eliminate the possibility of technical error. I phoned Kodak and asked about their Ektar film, explaining the magenta and sepia incidents.

In the first of two phone conversations, they asked if any of these off-color prints were connected to time exposures which might result in a color shift. I assured them that there were no exposures of over a fraction of a second, most of them with the camera being hand-held. At Kodak's request, I sent some of the negatives and prints so they could make an analysis. They chose to call me soon after the items were examined.

"The film is okay," they assured me.

"Then what causes the color changes?" I asked.

"All we can figure out," said the Kodak voice, "is that the filters in the lab needed changing. With Ektar film, they need changing more frequently than with other film."

I then explained that the same color deviation happened at three locations; Denver; Bozeman, Montana; and Sandpoint, Idaho...And wouldn't it be kind of unusual if all three labs needed their filters changed?

"Yes, but that's all we can figure out," concluded Kodak.

I thanked them and hung up. "Maybe they're right," said good old left brain, "since it always happens with Ektar." But "Magenta" was channeled in Bozeman. How do you explain that, L.B.?

The "Persephone incident" was unlike the Montana trip, even though it was an "almost" assignment, *almost* in the sense that I was asked to try to photograph Devic energies, but the energy I photographed was not the energy I was asked to photograph. Rene Schori asked me to take pictures of her raspberry bushes, where she sensed the energies, but I took a detour as soon as I entered her garden.

Rene lives just a few miles from us, and the day that I visited her — camera in hand — the weather was beautiful, the birds were singing, the sky was clear and the garden was at its peak. It was obvious that the Devas and Nature Spirits were joyfully doing their work and that Rene was in harmony with Nature's kingdom, growing outstanding flowers and vegetables planted in what I would term a free-style design. Behind the garden was a creek and a small waterfall.

As Rene directed me toward the raspberry bushes, I paused for a moment in front of a beautiful pink flower, a peony. It had a warm, vibrant, feeling, and its large, beautiful blossom was so heavy, the stem was bent almost double.

"I've got to take a picture of this peony first," I announced.

"Okay, let me hold up its head, so you can get a better shot" She did — and it was definitely a "better shot."

We then went to the raspberries, and Rene was right. There were energies in and around the raspberry bushes, showing up on the finished photo as a misty formation. But the real gift from the Devas was the energy of the peony, formed into the now-familiar flame shape, and it was blue — the first blue energy in my collection of energy formations on film.

A week later, Rene stopped by to see the print. Her immediate response was "Persephone."

"What?" my wife and I exclaimed almost simultaneously.

"Persephone."

"What does that mean?"

"I don't know. The word just came to me."

The encyclopedia defines Persephone as the Greek goddess of fertility, personifying the birth and decay of vegetation. Like everything we were experiencing, it all seemed to fit.

The energy formations are not seen with my physical eyes, nor am I consciously aware of seeing them with my inner vision, so the feeling that "this will be a light image"

"Persephone." Personifying the birth and decay of vegetation.

before I take the picture has never entered by conscious awareness. But there have been times, *after* it happened, when I was pretty sure I had photographed a Being of Light. The strongest feeling I ever had was in Glacier National Park in the summer of 1989.

Glacier is a wonderfully diverse and picturesque park, a photographer's playground. Situated in the northern Rockies near the Montana/Canadian border, the park offers breathtaking scenery, alpine lakes, conifer forests, rocky crags, roaring streams and all of the things visitors want to see and experience. As a result, most campgrounds are full during the height of the season — and that's when I was there.

The one campground I really liked on the west side of the Continental Divide had a fast flowing, cascading stream running right by it, and the best camping spot was understandably reserved for the disabled. But the volunteer in charge of the campground said if no disabled person arrived prior to 6:00 p.m., he would allow me to camp for one night in that space.

"Was this a little unusual?" I might have asked myself,

"Is there a reason this person — this volunteer I had never seen before — is going out of his way to make it possible for me to stay at this location? Is it because I'm *supposed* to be here?"

No disabled persons arrived that evening.

I set up camp and spent the rest of the evening scouting the area, taking some pictures of the stream and the cascading waters. I sat transfixed by the beauty and power of this roaring stream, the sound blocking out any conversations of passers-by. I closed my eyes and felt a wave of peaceful energy flowing through my body, my mind. My consciousness was carried by this stream, flowing over the rocks, around bends, riding up on sandbars, over logs, drifting as the waters misted above the stream, then plunging down again into the fast churning, swirling, rolling movement, tumbling joyfully through the gorges.

It seemed incredible to me that, in a place where humanity came to view in wonder, Nature in its purest form remained centered in its harmony with the Whole, seemingly unaffected by the trespassing human animals.

Perhaps, I mused, it is because those that walk these paths come to honor Nature, to be in tune with, to be a part of it. I returned to my campsite, allowing the peaceful, harmonious energies that I had experienced at the water's edge lead me into a sound sleep.

Early the next morning I hiked to a small alpine lake, sat on an ancient log by the shore, took some photographs, then found myself, once again, in a state of awe and wonder, admiring the beauty and grandeur of the mountains behind the lake. A thin, ribbon-sized stream fell out of the rocks part way down the mountain, cascading hundreds of feet to join other waters that had found the peace and quiet of this crystal-clear lake. The sky was cloudless, the air, crisp and pure. I felt thankful — thankful and fortunate to be able to experience this beauty.

On the trail back to camp, as I was about to cross a wooden footbridge, a chipmunk appeared, unafraid, probably accustomed to being in close contact with the human species. He stopped on the bridge, just feet ahead of me, tail

"Light Worker." It telepathically said, "That wasn't good enough — watch this."

twitching out some sort of message to the understanding animal world, as I focused my camera and took a picture. He paused, looked directly at me and telepathically conveyed the message, "That wasn't good enough, watch this." He then stood on his hind legs, reaching out for some buds on a small branch, and as his tiny front paws closed on the buds, I clicked the shutter once again. At that instant, I would have bet money there would be a light around his little body. There was, and it was a rose-colored light. I call him, "Light Worker."

I have never read anything about a multi-wave movement of energy, at least in my conscious recollection. But it seems to me we ride on — and in — several waves that move at different wave lengths. Once in a while, all of the waves seem to peak at the same moment and incredible things happen. Deep meditations are commonplace; our perception of life shifts to a more serene pattern; our life events take on an altered pattern of priorities; and we are able to interpret these events easily in an objective manner. As this state tends to subside, we realize it is a mental place we would like to return to. I have spoken to many who meditate and, without exception, these peaks seems to arrive in an unexpected manner, denying any plausible explanation and most always leaving the person with the question: "Why not *always?*" In the fall of 1989 I had such an experience, during a hike with Dawn.

We had hiked to the top of one of the mountains near our residences, then back down, and were hiking north along the easement road. As we walked, we were talking and admiring the fall leaves that were on the path, noticing the pattern they formed when they fell, noticing their various colors, their shapes, the different stems, their textures. As I looked down at the leaves, I suddenly felt I was walking *above* them, like I was three feet above the ground, but still *on the ground*. I was swept up into a state of euphoria, of absolute peace, transported by some magical space/time shift into a different reality.

Dawn, recognizing something strange was occurring, suggested I sit down. As I did, I saw waves of clouds moving under me, clouds like I had never seen before, clouds with a light, pinkish cast, and now I was passing through them — or they were passing through me — I couldn't tell, and it didn't matter.

Time didn't exist, there was no need for it, for there was no space to measure, no events that had to happen. The two of us moved on to a knoll, overlooking a clearing, surrounded by the forest. We sat down in this front-row seat of life on parade. All of creation was incredibly beautiful and clear, the grasses on the hillside rejoicing in their freedom with the wind helping them dance the joyful dance of life, the pines whispering their message of love and unison with All That Is, peaceful clouds moving gently over the mountain ridges, birds calling to their own species and to any others that would listen.

I felt like I was an observer and at the same time a joyful participant in this reality and simultaneously in others. It was a true feeling state, my senses expanding into a new and wonderful dimension. I could have spent an eternity in this incredible state of peace, and in some mysterious, abstract way, I did. It was "Satori," the Buddhist state of bliss.

When I returned home, Michael was immediately aware of my state, my "condition," by my eyes, which reflected the serenity of my being. The euphoria gradually — and regrettably — wore off. But the memory lingered, as well as some of the oneness that I experienced that remarkable fall day.

For the next month, it seemed that I was consistently open, attracting many invisibles to my conscious awareness, able to verbalize their thoughts, whether "they" were individuals or group consciousnesses. Many of these beings seemed to be drawn to me for specific reasons, others arrived, stayed a very short time, and left, like they were introducing themselves for a future contact. One short visit was made by Mesaba.

Since this time, I have a feeling that my guidance — whether one calls it a higher self, guides, inner knowing, or whatever — has put me out of reach of many of these entities. The reason I believe this happens is because the *real* answers lie within, not without; answers come from *me*, not from the invisibles. My truth is *my* truth, not another's, and although I have been guided in the past to listen to channeled information for specific purposes, some of which have been reviewed in this book. I now feel this is no longer appropriate for me to do.

While sitting in our living room one evening, a being spoke through me. The message was short, consisting of her name, Mesaba, and that she is the consciousness of an ancient African culture. It never occurred to ask what she was doing in north Idaho, but looking at it in a more cosmic perspective, the geographical location of any energy is not important to its message, nor to the time and space that we impose upon it. Mesaba would later be the subject of a beautiful photograph.

I was now carrying my camera with me most of the time when Dawn and I hiked, and shortly after my "peak experience," we walked to the beaver ponds, about three miles north or our properties. Hiking along a trail at the water's edge, as I crossed a large granite boulder, I involuntarily spoke the name, "Mesaba."

"Mesaba." An ancient African culture.

"Why did you say that?" questioned Dawn.

"It just came to mind — no reason."

No reason, indeed!

Mesaba had not been in my thoughts that day, nor had I expected to utter her name, but her energy was close at hand, so close, in fact, that when I pointed my camera across the pond and took a picture of what I thought was a colorful and peaceful scene, a beautiful being appeared on film. It was Mesaba, of course...

Chapter 5

—The Process—

Many of my pictures, which show energy formations, are the result of "mistakes," mistakes ranging from underexposure — and I have a goodly supply of these — to the impulsive clicking of the shutter "for no good reason." The underexposures sometimes render the photo unacceptable from a pure photographic standpoint, but often allow the Devic images to show more clearly, since they show themselves in white, gold, light blue and rose tones, contrasting with the dark, under-exposed background.

One of the more remarkable "for no good reason" shots was of my wife, at that time the only human to show an energy formation in any of the photographs that I have taken. I was in the meadow taking photos of our house to send to our friends in California, when Mike walked out the sliding glass door from the sun space, and seeing me taking pictures, tried to avoid being in the way. But "for no good reason," I took a photo of her — not the house — as she was stepping off the back stoop. From a logical viewpoint, there would be no reason whatsoever to take a picture of Mike while she was trying to get out of camera range, there would be no reason to take a picture of her instead of the original subject, and there would be no reason to expect a light image around a human, since it seemed, at that time, that humans were not a part of the Devic Kingdom.

Dave and Helen, our good friends from Escondido, were visiting us shortly after I took the picture of Mike trying to get out of the way of the camera. It was the first time they had visited us at our new home, and since Dave is a photographer and I wasn't sure how either of them would accept this unusual phenomenon, I purposely did not bring out my photos of energy formations, preferring to remain in the "Deva closet." However, Dave did accompany me to the photo dealer to pick up some prints, and a stealthy peek at my photos while leaving the store showed Mike in her *true* form, a bright, golden flame surrounding her body and extending above her head. Quickly putting the print back in the envelope, I wondered how I would ever explain this to Dave.

After we returned to the house, Dave sat with his back to the large windows which fill the south side of our living room. I nervously watched as he kept moving around in his chair, trying to find a better angle from which to view the 8" by 10" enlargement of "Dance of the Fairies," displayed on our bookcase.

Well, I thought, here it comes. Dave is sure going to ask me about that picture pretty soon, and I'm going to have to explain it.

Finally, Dave posed the question: "I've been looking at that picture for quite a while, thinking there might be a light reflection on the glass, but there is no reflection. What is it?"

"It's an energy formation that sometimes shows itself in my photos," I blurted out, thinking inwardly that the truth must sound more like fiction. Continuing on, I tried to explain what Devic energies are.

"Oh." Dave's comment was short and quick.

With that kind of — what I then considered — encouragement, I removed the photo of Mike from the photo store envelope, showed it to Dave and Helen, and waited.

Helen looked at it, saw the golden light around Mike's body, and with no further questions said, "We always knew she was special."

"Interesting," muttered Dave, and that was the end of the imagined inquisition.

So much for the fear of exposure.

With the availability of "channeled" information, one can become reliant, or dependent upon, the answers freely given by invisible intelligences through those who are capable and willing to provide this service. At one time, I was in awe of the persons who were able to do it, and of the astuteness these entities seemed to possess. Now, as I mentioned in the previous chapter, I feel that asking for channeled answers to my many questions about this process through another is, in a way, obstructing my being able to receive answers directly from within.

Back in the days when I read *Seth*, I had sent a note to Jane Roberts, Seth's channel, asking about any plans for releasing additional books. I received a handwritten answer from Jane, jotted on the top of a form letter. The form letter was dictated by Seth and was directed to persons who had asked for help in their personal lives. Although the letter did not apply to my inquiry, nor did I save it, I still vividly recall the message: "To those who have written for help, whether it be in the area of health of otherwise, *the answers you seek are within yourselves*, and if I had the power to solve your problems, I would not choose to, for doing so would deprive you of your own personal experience."

As humans progress, I feel we most of all need to trust *ourselves*; to trust the intuitive responses that we too often ignore, to trust our ability to bring forth the answers. By asking for outside help we are, in my opinion, limiting "direct" answers, ignoring our intuitive feelings, and sometimes bypassing the personal experiences that we need to help us evolve.

The last time I asked for channeled guidance was in September 1990, prior to my making my first "Beings of Light" public photo presentation. Although I was fairly certain about some aspects of my photographic endeavors, many of the answers to my questions were lingering in the transition zone — that area that is just outside of our mental acceptance but not buried in the deep recesses of our psyche. Specific answers were obscure, eluding my attempts to access them. Perhaps *attempting* is the reason that the answers were still out of reach.

I knew that, during my successful picture taking of Devic energies, I am first of all emotionally drawn to the subject. When this attraction occurs, it sets up a resonance between the subject and myself. I also knew that, in response to this resonance, the life force coalesces to take the form shown on the photographs. The question regarding the form

itself was temporarily eluding me. Were some of these energies in the form they show on film — but invisible to us — or
are all of them without form?

The information about the process, as described by Eay,
validated my feelings about the coalescence of the life force.
The information about form was originally to have been
included in this chapter, but in listening to the playback of
Eay on tape, it became clear that the philosophical manner
in which the information was related would not greatly
benefit the reader. If I were to sum up Eay's answer, it would
be like "yes and no." The beings that I photograph, in the
perception of Eay, are in form and are also formless. Form
and formless are identical in the sense that formlessness is
a condition, a state, and as such it becomes by definition,
form. Got it?

I feel that we, as humans, tend to equate consciousness
with form, but form is not necessary for consciousness to
exist. To deny the existence of all that is not seen by our
physical eyes is to deny the existence of oxygen, television
waves, electricity, wind, memory, thought, atomic particles,
love and much more.

I also feel that most of the energies I photograph have no
form. They are energy, and energy doesn't need form as we
know it. We need form to experience this corporeal existence,
but energies don't. Many are able to take form, however,
depending on the need and expectation of the humans with
whom they sometime connect, taking the form related to the
archetypes. For instance, some persons have seen fairies,
elves, gnomes, leprechauns, and I accept this as fact, even
though my experience in seeing other dimensional beings is
very limited. Our collective unconscious has formed a picture of what fairies, gnomes and others look like, and the
forms, when seen, appear as the archetype. So when the
picture of the fairies was impressed on one of my photos
("Dance of the Fairies"), the images matched the archetype of
fairies, gossamer wings and all. My belief that they don't have
form, like humans, doesn't make them any less real.

The big question, then, has to do with the origin of the
archetypes. Where did the archetype of a fairy come from?

Why do we accept the impression that they have wings and that they sparkle? It now appears likely to me that these beings once inhabited this dimension or that we, as humans, were able to see into theirs, and they were physical. If this is the case, and we carry this in our cellular memories, it would make for a good explanation.

In the summer of 1991, I was in our swing which is near our Deva sanctuary on the edge of the meadow. I was meditating, but it was one of the most unusual meditations I ever had. The meditation wasn't deep — it just happened when I closed my eyes. My intention was to enter the earth to visit — to connect with some of the beings that live there. Within seconds I was moving down through the earth.

I was on an escalator, like in a department store, the departure point just a few feet from where I sat on the swing. As I came to the end of my short downward ride, I was greeted by two of the most homely beings I had ever seen, either with my physical eyes or inner vision. They stood a maximum of four feet tall, were dressed in greenish brown clothing, wore hats that appeared to be dark green, and were smiling an ear-to-ear toothless grin, the center of their round faces accommodating large, bulbous noses. They were beautiful...and they were full of joy!

Their duty, it seemed, was to greet people who arrived from...wherever. They helped me step off the escalator, like little hosts, but no words were spoken. As I stepped onto the cobblestone, or perhaps brick street, I was aware of many humans, or at least human-like persons, walking in and out of buildings, the architecture of which closely resembled Mediterranean. The village square, where I arrived, was most colorful with a variety of flowers planted along the walkways. The sky was like an earth sky when there is a slight overcast, illuminating the area with a pleasant, diffused light, and as I observed this sky, I was aware that the light was provided by the entities in that space. It was, in fact, Universal energy, manifested as light.

It was a pleasant visit, even though no one acknowledged my presence except the gnomes. I'll go back again sometime, and maybe take my camera.

A lot has happened since that visit to Montana in the spring of 1989. A lot has been made more clear to me through intuitive feelings and "a little help from my friends." The trip to Montana was to show me that "trying" to take the energy photos negates the process. I found it is a kind of thoughtless act: not trying, not expecting, not anticipating. Now, when I pick up my camera, the purpose is to enjoy the emotional experience of being in Nature, of seeing the beauty of the small things that exist on this marvelous planet, to pay attention to the wonders that surround us, and to try, in the best manner I can, to transmit this experience to a small piece of film. If in this activity I produce some unusual photographs, it becomes a bonus.

One of the earlier attempts to "create" a picture occurred in the summer of 1988. Five of us, Gayl, Dawn, Peggy, Mike and myself, gathered in our meadow one summer day for the purpose of raising our vibrations, tuning into the energies. And when this attunement was at its peak, I was to take a photograph, the theory being that we should really get an image with our collective consciousnesses in sync. It was a grand idea.

We sat in a large circle and through the process of group meditation, we mentally invited the Devic energies to be seen on film. I had never tried to meditate and take a picture except at Clarstar Farms in Montana, and there I worked alone. Perhaps this time, with five of us putting forth our best vibrations, we would get some super images.

I took three or four pictures while we were in the circle, then Gayl and Dawn went their own way, both of them drawn toward a small ravine just west of the house. They sat together, while the rest of us stayed on the periphery, not wanted to disturb their efforts and break their concentration. When they both saw, with their inner vision, a pulsing, shimmering light in the area, they called me to take a picture. At the very instant I snapped the shutter, they both agreed the light was at its apex, and excitedly exclaimed, almost in unison, "You got it."

I didn't get it.

When the prints came back, the only faint energy that

showed was one of the meadow shots, taken before their silvery image appeared.

Another organized attempt to photograph Devas was at the request of Carolyna and Harry Green. The Greens, who resided in Sandpoint, had a crystal room where they displayed their crystals and sold them to interested people. Carolyna was very active in teaching about the healing power of crystals, was very much in tune with crystal energy, and both she and Harry had sensed the presence of a crystal Deva many times. This should be easy — we already knew the Deva was there — so it was just a matter of getting in tune with her and taking the pictures, right?

I set up my camera on a tripod in their crystal room, the three of us got into a meditative state, and I took four or five photographs. When the prints came back from the lab, we had some real nice pictures of crystals. No Deva, not even a glimmer...Just pictures of crystals.

The next visit, two months later, produced one very clear energy formation, and two others with less intensity. It is still not entirely clear to me as to the reason for one failure and one success in the same location, same crystals, same Devic energies. My assumption is that the energies were not open to us for reasons of their own (as if they needed reasons) and that possibly we were not at the right intersection of the energy wave curve, which I feel might have a strong bearing on the success rate of this kind of endeavor.

In one instance, the circumstances surrounding the photographing of a bear appeared to be a set-up. It was in the fall of 1989, and a borrowed massage table sat directly in front of the sliding glass door in the living room, For reasons that are now clear but were then obscure, I had, for the first time, laid my camera on this table. The sequence of events was astounding, and I feel Andrea had orchestrated the whole event with a black bear.

Here's the scenario...

Andrea was communicating with the bear and said, "Look, bear, I want you to stand on your hind legs at the edge of the meadow, and when Mike walks out on the deck, sees you at your full height, she will turn and say, 'Oh, my God,'

"Black & Light." This bear appeared "accidentally" the first time I left my camera on the massage table.

and re-enter the house. Orin will be coming through the living room at this precise moment, will pick up his camera and take two exposures. The first one will be best, being closer, so be sure to turn your head for a profile — otherwise, you might look like a big, black dog."

The first exposure showed a bluish white light formed around the body and extending upward into the flame-shape. I named this picture "Black and Light."

The second exposure showed a black something going over a downed tree.

The Arden story is different. It revolves around another Being of Light, only this one is human. Arden, the daughter of my wife's best friend, had just graduated from college, knew of her parent's planned visit to our Idaho home, and drove from Seattle during this period to simultaneously see her parents and visit us. Although Arden was changed physically, her sensitivity, as I remembered it from when she was eight years old, remained intact, undiluted, unconcealed, in spite of growing up.

While living in Escondido, we were visited one summer by eight-year-old Arden, her parents, and 5,000 uninvited flies, flies that came in out of the heat and took naps on our ceiling, flies that buzzed around, got on food, spotted the windows, and woke one up from a summer's afternoon nap.

Our method of disposing of these pests, the neatest (for us) and quickest, was to vacuum them from the ceiling. Arden, seeing me do this, left the room crying, followed by Dick, her father, who was told through sobs, "Flies have just as much right to live as we do."

At that time, I would not allow thoughts like *that* to become a conscious part of my reality. I would not permit *that* kind of sensitivity to surface, lest I be considered weak, unmanly, unprepared to go forth with my shield and sword, doing battle in the business world, fighting off all the potential dragons of the day. But now...now the priorities in my life have nothing to do with making war on insects, competitors, the establishment, the IRS or political opponents, and it seems it was important to remember, for 15 years, how a sensitive child cared for living things.

Arden and I hiked to the beaver ponds on her first day with us that summer. I wasn't quite sure what to expect from this person whom I hadn't seen for so many years, this adult whom I remembered as a child, this grown-up walking at my side. If I had any doubts concerning her awareness, her sensitivity, they were dispelled when she stopped, held a wild flower, and told it how beautiful it was.

I told her I was proud that she still displayed the sensitivity I remembered her for, how great it was that she communicated with the flower.

"I don't communicate with them, I just appreciate them," she remarked.

"When you connect with a flower like you just did, you are communicating," I assured her, explaining that communication need not be verbal, but that feelings are the true measure of communication.

We had a great hike that summer day.

The following day, Arden and I walked to the river, just minutes away from our house, where she walked along the shore alone, as I sat on a little beach next to the railroad trestle that crosses the river.

Later she returned, walking aimlessly up the grade to the trestle, then she ventured out onto the part that spans the water. After walking halfway to the other shore, I watched her as she turned and headed back in a preoccupied state, carefully stepping on the railroad ties, letting her thoughts take her mentally elsewhere, letting her body consciousness find its way back to the end of the trestle, then stepping onto the ground and descending the small hill. It was then that I picked up my camera, saw her through the lens, and took the picture.

Our thoughts precede all action, moving faster than light, preparing our way to where we are going, forming a path that we then fill in. Arden's thoughts, when she saw she was about to descend the small hill after leaving the trestle, formed a molecular path to her destination. She then filled in this path, and I took a picture of her during this process.

As I took the picture, Arden was not quite where I thought I saw her, but, in fact, was a little short of that location. When the shutter opened and closed, the camera picked up the light body of Arden, preceding her physical body by about one-half step. The print showed a beautiful silver light surrounding Arden's physical body. She was the second human to show the light for my camera.

We have all heard the expression, "letting go," many times, and when someone says, "Just let go," or "allow," or "release," my reaction is like a golfer who is told to relax while in the backswing. So, if I were to try to outline this process of multi-dimensional photography in order to instruct another person in the technique, I would just have to say, "Don't *try.*"

My best pictures — that is, the more clear energy photos — have been taken "by accident." Emotion, feeling-state, harmony, and "openness" come to mind when I attempt to describe my state of mind during these successful events. But there have been many times when I enjoyed all of these virtues and the energy formations didn't appear on the film. Obviously, I don't have all of the answers yet, or I could, among other things, explain about the turkeys.

Wild turkeys visited our land and our neighbors' land for three years, coming in the early spring and leaving just before the snow fell. The turkeys don't visit us any more due to the actions of a well-intentioned but misinformed elderly lady who lived a mile to the west of our property, and who believed the turkeys carried salmonella, causing some of the songbirds that she fed to die. Too late we learned that her failure to keep the bird feeders clean was the reason for the death of the songbirds, not our friends the turkeys. Too late, because she had already convinced the Idaho Fish and Game Department to trap and move the turkeys.

The turkeys mated on our land, the toms gobbling and showing their beautiful plumage as they strutted, stiff-legged, calling for the hen's attention. Then, each spring after mating, the hen would disappear, make her nest in the nearby forest, hatch her eggs and proudly bring her babies to show us. The turkey babies were so small that their location would have been unknown by us except for the tell-tale movement of the short grasses in the meadow and near our deck, as these little birds struggled to keep within range of their mother, listening for the hen's clucking as she called, sometimes scolding, sometimes sounding an alert and spreading her wings to cover her brood if a hawk or other large bird was in the area.

It was a unique and joyful experience to be so close to these wild birds, having them trust us, allowing us to approach within a few feet as we offered them sunflower seeds; watching their first attempted flight, first running full speed along the ground, then flapping their little wings in a frantic attempt to become airborne; marveling at the hen's instincts as she taught them how to select the right food, where to find the bugs, what vegetation would sustain them.

In the spring of 1990, the sad part was watching the flock decline from twelve little energetic bundles of life to eleven, then nine then eight, seven, six and finally, at the end of the season, just five were left — the survivors of a very wet spring and active predators. We had to remind ourselves that Nature works this way, that the strong survive, if we leave them alone. But hearing the hen's plaintive clucking, the unmistakable call of a worried mother, and then to find one less baby returning because of a hungry coyote or hawk, was difficult for us to forget. The hen's acceptance of this, what one might refer to as harsh reality, however, gave us cause to reflect on the wondrous, accepting manner in which non-human animals move through their existence, not wondering what happened, not looking back and feeling loss or feeling cheated, but following their evolutionary path, knowing that all is well.

During our "turkey" years, I find it interesting that the humans that live in this same geographical space, our neighbors, were completely non-threatening to the turkeys. Not one person hunted them, not one person wanted to see them in danger, not one person wished them any harm, including the lady that had them trapped and moved 15 miles away.

I must have more turkey pictures than most families do baby pictures. I took roll after roll of turkey shots: the toms during their courtship, strutting and posturing for the hen; the small babies trying to find their way through the four-inch-high grass; turkeys in the meadow, in the garden; the hen with her brood; the statue-like poses when they felt danger was imminent; our cats with the turkeys; on and on went the photos and the videos.

In all of these pictures, not one energy formation showed itself around or near the turkeys, not one subtle energy, no light, nothing. It is conceivable, as my wife said, that they were so concerned about survival, so concerned about the predators, that they would not take some of their life force and project it into light, and that is a distinct possibility. Another possibility is that our vibrational energy patterns were not harmonious, not compatible, not meaning better or worse, higher or lower, just not compatible.

After 40 pictures of Big Horn rams in Jasper National Park, Canada, in 1990, after feeling so close, and being so physically close to them, after being emotionally drawn to those beautiful creatures in that extraordinary setting, one barely noticeable light showed up on one print, and that was all. Those guys weren't concerned about survival. They had never been hunted, and I approached within 35 yards of them. But the same day I took Light-Being photos of a Marmot, and many lights showed from the majestic mountains nearby.

At the other end of the scale, however, there is Guinevere, one of our cats. About one-half or more of the pictures I have taken of her have a light around her body or nearby. One shows a beautiful funnel, a vortex of energy coming from her heart. I have pictures of her sitting on the deck, hiding in the bird feeder, all with light. I do have an exceptionally close relationship with this loving animal, and our vibrations are definitely compatible. But I also felt a strong connection with the turkeys, and the rams.

One of the most common questions during my slide presentations is, "Do you always use the same camera?" For a long time I was unable to answer, "No," to this question. Then in the fall of 1990, I made a trial run north to Bonners Ferry, then to northwestern Montana and tried out a Canon EOS camera that I had purchased as a Christmas present for Mike. The camera can be used as a fully automatic or a manual, and knowing Mike would prefer auto-everything, I set out for a day of automatic fun.

It was a beautiful fall day, the leaves of the birch trees were turning, the air was crisp, there were a few puffs of cumulus clouds hovering above the Cabinet Wilderness area in Montana, and it seemed a perfect day for a camera try-out.

Two rolls of film were exposed that day, using the various modes the camera offered: close-ups, scenic, depth of field choices. I took pictures of Timothy Grass along the road, road signs with mountain back-drops, streams, wetlands, trees, meadows, not thinking "energy formations" or whether the beings would choose to show, but just trying out the camera so I could verbally relate to Mike how this potentially intimidating auto-camera worked, how simple it really was.

When the prints came back from the processing lab, on the second roll, halfway through, a subtle but distinct energy appeared in the middle of a meadow. I could now answer, "Yes," to the question about other cameras. The fact that the image appeared after about 40 or more exposures is in accordance with the usual delay which occurs when I buy a new lens or try a different kind of film. I feel this delay is due to an adjustment needed by the intelligences to accommodate the new device or film that is of a different vibrational frequency.

My impression is that the process, that is, the *technical* process of this type of photography involves two interrelated vibrational phenomena: the first is a "beat frequency" that takes place *outside* the camera; the second is a step-down of the vibrational frequencies that takes place *inside* the camera.

From what some engineers have told me, a *beat frequency* occurs when two frequencies are transmitted or activated, and under certain conditions create a third frequency, a by-product of the other two. As an example, if there is one frequency of 300,000 cycles per second, and another of 200,000 cycles, the beat frequency would be the sum of the two, or 500,000, divided by two, or 250,000 cycles per second.

My totality, as yours, consists of a certain vibrational frequency; the subject I am photographing has another frequency. The beat frequency that is established between the two is what enters the lens of the camera. This frequency is far above the human eye's ability to register, so it needs to be stepped down to the visible light spectrum by the energies working within the camera. This is what is "seen" by the film.

Continuing with this possible explanation, there would be some vibrational patterns that would produce a frequency not compatible to mine, limiting or negating the camera's ability to pick it up in the form of light. This would account for the reason that some species don't show light images on film.

As mentioned earlier, the energies within the camera also must make adjustments each time something new is added, which would explain why there is always a delay as the step-down process is being reconfigured to accommodate the new frequencies in another lens, different film, or in the case of Mike's Christmas present, a new camera.

The above explanation is, as I mentioned, my impression. This impression subject to correction, verification or substitution.

Chapter 6

—The Unbusiness—

I *really* retired when we moved to Idaho, never yearning for the "good old days" of business, so when Michael — the same Michael that just happened to arrive the day my first prints were spread out on the coffee table — approached me about distributing my photographs, I resisted for more than a couple of reasons. I didn't want the negatives to be turned over to another person or company. I didn't want the prints to be distributed without some kind of attached explanation. I didn't want to advertise, establish outlets, extend credit. In other words, I didn't want to go into business. It was now early fall 1989.

Michael told me he traveled around the northwest, would also be going to Arizona for the winter, would be able to contact New Age bookstores in his travels, and could set up dealers for me.

Okay, so I could eliminate the credit problem by selling for cash only, I could let Michael set up dealers, eliminating the need to advertise, and this would take care of a large part of my objections concerning going into business. But I was still concerned about how the pictures would be handled. If I just *sold* the prints, it would allow too much latitude for interpretation as the story passed from me to Michael to the dealer and consumer, eroding the meaning of the individual light images in the photographs.

Prior to this time, I had sent some of my photos to Gayl, who showed them at her various workshops in the Northwest, and I knew she was clear in her explanation of what the light images were, but Michael's proposal was a lot different, and it allowed for great latitude in interpretation as the photos passed through several hands.

There was something else that had to be done; there was something missing. I told Michael the distribution of photos just didn't seem right, and I would contact him when and if I was able to resolve my concern.

I allowed the idea of distribution to languish in the foyer of my mind for a couple of weeks, permitting it to rest when it wanted to, letting it come out for a visit occasionally. Gradually, the distribution idea took shape, and I phoned Michael for another get-together.

At our meeting, I explained that there needed to be a story told in print about the various beings that I was photographing, so that there was less chance of distortion of the story, that perhaps the prints could be attached to a card, like a note card, that I didn't want him or anyone else, as a partner, but that I would be the manufacturer and he could be a distributor. I further explained that the reason I would be doing this would not be financial gain, but for the purpose of expanding our human perception, offering validation to those that believe in unseen intelligences and setting the door of awareness ajar for others.

Now it appeared we were on the way to distribution, except for the words needed to explain these unique energy formations that showed up on the processed film. The story had to be uncomplicated, truthful, conveying a message and a meaning. I soon learned that *that* part was not an easy task.

I selected ten of the photographs which showed the most obvious energy formations, the ones that wouldn't take a lot of explaining to the general public — showing the flame shape surrounding animals, crystals, mountains, plants. After they were chosen, I felt there should be an explanation of what each energy formation represented, and if they had names, how the names came into being and what was the background of each scene.

The explanation of the image of Andrea would be quite simple; the fairies in "Dance of the Fairies" would also be relatively simple compared to an explanation of how an ancient African culture (Mesaba) was connected with north Idaho, what it was doing here, and why. Other photos were also very difficult to put into a category.

My wife Mike and I worked on this project for two days, independently writing our explanations of the individual energy formations, showing what we came up with to the other person, and discussing it. Nothing was working. No explanations were right. Something was definitely missing — plus I had the feeling that the buyers of the cards would more than likely have their own interpretations, be drawn to certain energies. To present them with a patent explanation of what they were looking at would short-circuit their own valuable intuitive impressions.

At the end of the second day, I put aside the project and went to Sandpoint. It just wasn't coming together. No matter how hard we tried, our best creative efforts ended up in the wastebasket. We were either trying to complicate a simple process, or simplify a complex one, I wasn't sure, so I climbed into my truck with errands in mind, jiggled over the three-quarters of a mile of bumpy road, entered Highway 2 and turned east toward Sandpoint.

It never occurred to me that the answer would come while driving, but now that I understand a little more about this process of "letting go," it seems likely that the answer would not have come if I had continued to try to *make* it happen, for this would be putting expectation and timing into the equation, and letting go means just...letting go. I was approaching Dover, almost to the railroad overpass, and the little voice arrived in my head, not loud, but very clear: "Write a verse." The message was emphatic, as if this were *the* solution. The verse would not be to explain just *one* energy, the same verse would appear on the back of *all* the cards. The message would be appropriate for all "Beings of Light," and would eliminate the need to create a story or an explanation for each individual card.

I finished my errands, drove back home, sat down and wrote the verse in a few minutes. I am still moved by the words, the meaning, that is conveyed in it.

Our lights, though seen by many,
Are recognized by few.
Like a dream, whose memory fades upon awakening,

Our forms seem fleeting,
Darting into memory's shadows.
Allow yourselves to believe, to feel, to know
That we, like you, are Beings of Light.
We share with you the joy of love —
The joy of life.

The cards have literally found their way into many homes in many states since this beginning. Although the numbers are relatively small compared to Hallmark or other card companies, the Light that travels with them, spreading from home to home, state to state, is much greater than anyone can imagine, and I sense that these cards are seldom thrown away, most likely being kept on one's desk, mantle, dresser, wall or refrigerator door.

At this writing, certain inmates of a Federal prison have requested cards, after being shown one by a sister inmate, and posters hang in many healing centers, massage therapists' and psychic readers' offices, private homes — all bringing Light to those who enter and feel harmonious with the projected energy, and it makes me feel good, especially when the cards or posters are delivered by a conduit.

A gallery and frame shop in Sandpoint, The Art Hang-Up, is a dealer who carries my cards and who had a poster of "Persephone" until recently, when the poster's healing purpose and its ultimate location became clear.

Two ladies who entered The Art Hang-Up, were taken by the poster of "Persephone," the peony, but *couldn't see the blue light,* the energy formation, that extended from the center of the flower to the top of the enlargement. They bought the poster and asked Patty to frame it for them. But here's the neat part: Had they *seen* the blue light, according to Patty, they wouldn't have accepted that it was, in fact, the photograph of an invisible intelligence, and they wouldn't have purchased it, since their mind-set was such that they would not be open to it.

But here's the really neat part...One of the ladies' mothers was in a convalescent home, and the poster was purchased for her. So, these two dear, unsuspecting ladies were a conduit for the Light that is being spread, not only to the mother, but to all the patients and nurses at the convalescent home. What a wondrous example of how the Universe works!

When I say that the cards and posters have literally found their way into the right hands, this means that I have allowed the distribution to take its own direction, that most of the exposure has been through first-hand introduction at locations such as the EXPO, group presentations, or word-of-mouth, where those who see them and resonate with the images, the messages, take the cards home where they kept and/or mailed them to friends.

In September 1990, I came out of the "Deva closet" in Sandpoint, and I made my first "Beings of Light" slide presentation at the Gardenia Center, a non-denominational, non-sectarian meeting place, supported by some very dedicated, aware and service-oriented people. I printed some flyers, and I put them up at laundry mats, the mall, on the downtown kiosk, and I stopped at the newspaper to ask if they would put the information in their weekly calendar of events. To my surprise, the scheduled presentation *did* appear in the calendar section of the paper, and the lady who handles the calender listing for the paper was the first one to show up on the evening of my "light show." Another surprise was that 50 people showed up, many of whom were not involved in any kind of metaphysical goings-on. This was perfect, this blending of people, some of whom knew invisible intelligences existed and wanted to see the photos and also those who were on the fringes, plus others who were curious, maybe seeking and/or skeptical, but for whom I might open the door of awareness at least a little way.

I felt good about the presentation and being able to share my slides and the information with others. I was not interested in converting disbelievers; I was not trying to convince anyone of anything. This made the presentation easy, and the questions that were asked were not in the least challenging, even though I would not have been concerned had the questions been of a skeptical nature. It was a new experience for me, *not* trying to teach, *not* trying to show the audience techniques, methods, short-cuts and advantages as I did when I taught my real estate seminars. It was fun, and I felt an energy lift as I progressed through the slides, reliving the events that surrounded the wonderful, unbelievable experiences of connecting with the world of Nature, the Devic Kingdom.

Prior to the presentation at the Gardenia Center, I took a trip to Spokane and had "Dance of the Fairies" enlarged to a sixteen-inch by twenty-inch poster, put it in a frame, and subsequently showed it to my first public audience. At that time it was unclear why I would do an enlargement, and I don't remember if it was Mike or Dawn who suggested how it might look blown up, or if I just wanted to see a larger image. But immediately following my first slide presentation, I was able to exhibit my cards and show what a poster looked like. I held up the framed enlargement so all could see. Two days later, I received a phone call from a lady who had attended, asking if she could purchase a poster-size enlargement of the fairies.

Back in my business days, I would have made a cost break-down, defined the profit required, made a resale price projection, calculated ad costs and overhead, and blah, blah, blah. But those days were *truly* behind me. All I was able to offer to this caller was that it cost me $25 to have it done, I had to make a 150-mile round trip to Spokane, and — not trusting the mail or a courier to safely deliver the negative — I had to spend the day waiting for the lab to do the enlargement.

As I explained all of this, it became clear that it would not be feasible to have it done in this manner. But I did take her name and phone number, just in case, unaware that there were forces at work.

For the next couple of months nothing happened, until I suddenly became "interested" in doing posters, sent bids to photo labs in Seattle and Spokane — the two places within driving distance — so I could hand-deliver the negatives and avoid the risk of losing them in the mail. But if Seattle was the most competitive, it still was 350 miles away and required a two-day trip for each batch of posters, added more cost to the project, and required a long-term projection of sales to save frequent Seattle excursions.

One firm in Seattle had a good price, providing there was no "cropping," no change from a horizontal to vertical format, for example. This meant that my "Dance of the Fairies" and some others would not be able to be done at these good prices. This whole thing was beginning to sound too much like a business venture — that is, until another "cooperative incident" was born into existence.

The Light magazine's home office is in Olympia, Washington, and Bill Koopman, the editor, and his wife, were given some of my cards by Pamela Chase and Jonathan Pawlick, the authors of *Trees for Healing*, mentioned previously. Jonathan and Pamela had been buying my cards for over a year, but we had never met, until I visited EXPO '90, in Seattle, at which time we arranged a meeting at their home. I shared with them about an hour and a half of photographic experiences related to the Devic Kingdom. Shortly after I returned to Idaho, a letter from Pamela and Jonathan arrived, and included in the envelope was a sample issue of *The Light* and an invitation from the editor saying that he would be interested in doing a photo essay in one of his forthcoming issues. This is where the cooperative incident comes in.

In order to provide a publicity-quality photograph of myself to use in the article, I purchased a roll of black and while film, and with Mike playing photographer, all 24 shots were exposed, we thought. But when I rewound the film, the ease with which the rewind crank turned told me that I had not engaged the sprocket well enough for the film to be advanced with each shot.

My usual source for developing told me they did not do their own black-and-white processing, and it would require a couple of weeks — two weeks of waiting to find out if I had any good exposures. I didn't have that kind of time, so they referred me to another local lab.

Strange little incidents started piling up. The lab I was referred to planned on leaving on vacation that day, were delayed by weather, so agreed to process my roll on the next day, Saturday. Saturday morning I discovered my fears were justified — there was one exposure, an unusable one, on the roll.

It was *Yellow Pages* time, and sure enough, Snappy's 1-hour photo place did black-and-white work.

There is more chasing around to the story. I bought another roll of black and white and had Snappy's develop it, only to find the photos didn't look publicity-quality to me. Then Dave, the owner of Snappy's, took my portrait and processed it while I waited. It was at this point, mostly out of a desire to generate conversation than really caring about his business, that I mentioned how surprised I was that they processed black-and-white film.

"Oh, sure, we're a 'can do' place," he quipped.

"What else can you do?" I queried.

"Just about anything."

"You don't do posters, do you?"

"Sure do."

"Sixteen-by-twenty-inch enlargements?"

"Yep."

Not only could he do posters, but he would be able to crop, do touch-ups if the emulsion wasn't spot-free on the blow-ups, was competitive with the out-of-town labs, and the negatives could be hand-delivered by me, reducing the possibility of loss to a minimum!

All this running around, not loading film right, vacations, *Yellow Pages* follow-up, "accidental" conversations, the need for Bill to have a publicity shot which he never used — led me to the poster place. Will wonders never cease? I hope not...

Chapter 7

—*The Unending*—

The photographic phenomenon, the photographing of unseen energies, is a process that never becomes boring, never seems to stay quite the same, although until recently I could count on two basic shapes, the flame shape and the vortex or funnel shape. In the summer of 1991, some of the images surprised me with a new series of shapes and colors.

My camera always seems to be nearby during, or just before, the full moon, and I quite often photograph energy formations during this period. The first very unusual shape that showed up was a near full moon in, I believe, August. The photo was taken with the camera mounted on a tripod to steady it, but the print shows what appeared to be movement, giving the moon a kind of double-bodied look. But in the lower portion of the picture, a blue energy appeared in a cone shape.

Another photo looked like Casper, the ghost, as he was leaving planet Earth, self-propelled, of course, and other photos of the moon showed the now-familiar fairy at the bottom of the picture, but minus the usual flame that normally extends to the top of the picture.

With rare exception, my moon photos are taken on clear nights with no clouds in the sky, and if there are clouds, I never seem to get an energy formation in the photo. In the fall of 1991 on a clear night, I took a full moon photo. But when the print came back, it showed the moon surrounded and shrouded in a very fine mist of aqua and rust tones, and it came with an energy that I immediately sensed was an angelic being. This was a surprise to me, since I am not normally thinking of angels, talking about angels, or in any way associating my pictures with angelic beings.

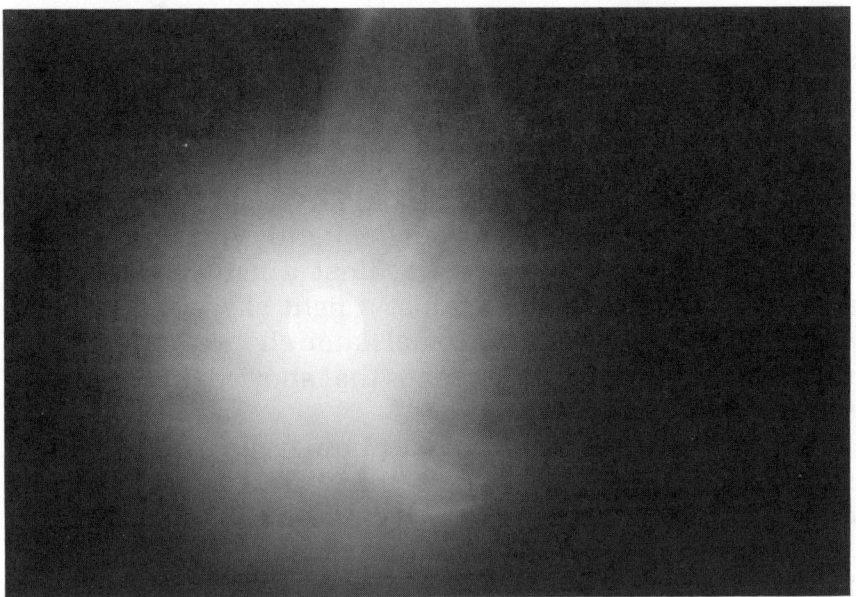

"Angelica." Taken on a clear night, an angelic presence became visible.

The reason angels don't enter my consciousness, I recently discovered, is due to my early exposure to the Christian teachings in my grandparents' home where I was raised, where God was punishing, always watching to see that one did good, and the angels, of course, were God's messengers. Having rejected the concept of a personalized, vindictive God many years ago, I kind of tossed out the angels, too, feeling they were part of the system that I no longer wanted to be a part of.

It wasn't until after I took this picture, and communicated with my friends, Pamela Chase and Jonathan Pawlick, that I realized how I had cleverly omitted the word, "angel," when presenting my slides, always explaining that Devas are "Beings of Light" or "Shining Ones." When Pamela reminded me that Devas, in their perception, are synonymous with angels, this unconscious belief was brought to the surface.

When extra prints were made of this particular photo, I sent one to Gayl in Montana, who called immediately to ask for a poster of it and said she had received the name, "Angelica," and did that mean anything to me.

In the earlier stages — one might say the developmental stages — of my surprise gift, the gift of bringing light into this dimension through photography, and as I became more skilled in seeing the subtleties in the photographs, I noticed that many pictures had been impressed with energy, but that the identification of the energy could be easily overlooked at first. Misty, fog-like images were frequently visible in some of the photos, others that were against a light background, such as a mountain top against a light sky, would not be seen, and in addition to the usual flame shapes and funnels, there were, occasionally, energies that showed themselves in other forms.

I was ready to throw out one photograph of a tree with a squirrel in it because it was so "bad," but as could now be expected, the right person arrived at the right moment and suggested that there was indeed a strong energy in the photo. Further investigation showed what appeared to be an archetype of Pan, the mythical (?) Greek god — and I almost threw it away!

One of the most interesting comments I can remember came from Joi, the star in the "Dance of the Fairies" picture. One evening Dawn and Ray joined us, and a shy, sweet voice spoke through Dawn as she opened to channel. I intuitively felt it was one of the fairies in the photograph, one who had never connected with humans before.

"Why are you not honest with one another?" this sweet voice asked.

"What do you mean?" I replied, defensively.

"When you speak, you are not always open from the heart, and if you are not open, we cannot see you."

I knew *we* couldn't see *them* if we were not open, but never dreamed that *they* cannot see *us* unless we were in that state.

For a long period of time, if I am consciously aware of being in touch with what I would term my cosmic self, I see a crystal blue color while in meditation. Many times I am aware of some blue, and if I am *really* connected, I am immersed in this beautiful blue color. When this happens, a surge of energy and warmth often flows through my body; a

"Dance of the Fairies." Joi, visible in the lower portion of this photo, says, "If you are not open and honest with one another, we cannot see you."

feeling of well-being accompanies the sensation of being one with my totality. These times are very special to me, very important to the part of me that needs validation, reassurance that I am more than the reflection I see in the mirror each day.

The crystal-blue phenomenon is directly related to the blue that now appears in some of the photographs, starting with Persephone, who expressed herself in a blue flame and was subsequently followed by a number of other blue energy formations, some with a rose-colored light. Part of the explanation for these phenomena was given to me by Eay, part came to me, and it feels right, so I'll pass it on.

The blue of my cosmic self, in some instances, integrates with the energy of the subject and permeates the light images. I honestly am not sure at my conscious level why the integration takes place some times and not others, but I feel that my totality, including my cosmic self, comes into phase or peaks at certain times, allowing the color integration when the wave is at this peak, and as it wanes, the energy penetra-

"Deer." Andrea's rose-colored energy integrated with the deer's, demonstrating that her energies assisted in this photo.

tion is less intense. The rose tones represent Andrea's color, signifying harmony and gentility. As she assists me in some of these photographs, her color sometimes is incorporated, also riding on the energy surges, just as my color blue does. In one instance, both colors, rose and blue, appeared in two different photos of the same subject. It happened in Boulder, Colorado.

In May of 1990, while visiting our good friends Brent and Patty in Lyons, the four of us drove the 30 miles to Boulder. Brent went to get his eyes checked at a clinic while Patty, Mike and I walked to the U.S. Bureau of Standards, less than a block away.

As we entered the building, my attention was drawn to a large, 440-pound quartz crystal, brought to the U.S. from Madagascar, which was on prominent display in this extremely busy lobby. Conference rooms, located right off the lobby, were overcrowded with meeting-goers and the many people taking advantage of short breaks to use the public phone right next to this crystal. There were visitors walking by, and great human activity surrounded the crystal. It was not exactly what you would consider a place of peace and relaxation, but I had the time, the tripod, the camera and the film, so why not!

I took two photos, one with a telephoto and one with a 50 mm lens. When the prints were developed, two subtle energies were apparent, one on the left side of the crystal in exposure #1 and one on the right side in #2. One was rose; one was blue. Two surprises all at once: energies showing themselves in this kind of an environment, and both exposures including energy formations, but in two colors.

I said it before, but trying to take photos of energy formations seldom produces them — whether the subject is animal, vegetation, or crystal, no matter what my mood is, how strongly I sense the energies, how sunny and/or beautiful the day is.

Mike and I drove to a barter fair north of Sandpoint, taking some circulated silver coins that I had purchased for barter a year or so earlier, "just in case" our nation experienced an economic disaster. This was in the early spring of 1989, and I was feeling less and less like we would need these coins , as I began to realize that the Universe seems to take care of us, gradually understanding the dependency that these coins engendered, what they represented.

We were drawn to one booth displaying gemstones of all kinds, including a large assortment of quartz crystals that wanted to go home with us. This booth was run by a man and wife who understood the value of the silver coins we offered in trade. The movement of the coins to their hands set in motion a desire to dispose of the balance of the coins as soon as we returned home, releasing the need to hold onto them, understanding more fully the value of energy movement, making space for more influx into our lives.

The next morning, I put all of these newly acquired gems in mesh sacks, the kind that onions and oranges come in, and hiked to a special stream that runs through the woods about a mile from our home. The stream is seasonal, and this time of the year it ran with great energy, flowing around granite boulders, cascading over downed trees, through secret passageways only to appear from under rocks and brush and logs a little farther downhill. I sat next to this crystal-clear, cold stream and felt in complete harmony with these surroundings. It brought to my mind the vague but exciting feeling that I had existed in times past as a conscious partner with Nature, knowing, without effort, the oneness of all things, the unity that exists in the consciousness of all things. I sat there, enthralled with the simplicity of being and the joy of living, admiring the animals and birds that inhabited this area, opening my heart to all of Nature, feeling the inner beauty of this experience. As I sat there, permeated by this feeling, I was reminded that the creatures of the forest never wonder who they are, what their purpose is — *they know*. They find no need to search for their connection in the Universe, their part in the harmony of all things. As I sat there that beautiful spring day in north Idaho, I thought, Why am I not always like this, how can I find such peace, such inner joy, in *this* spot *this* time, but not *every* time?

The crystals were receptive to the cleansing in this cold stream; they tumbled in the mesh sacks for a couple of hours, which cleansed them of any residual energies that might not be compatible to our own. They rolled and turned as the cascades flowed over and under them, as the clear water — run-off from the spring's melting snows — purified them as well as allowing them to be in contact with another of Earth's elements. I meditated as their energies clearly exuded joy and harmony, immersing myself in this special experience with them, alone, unencumbered by human thought or reaction.

A few days later, I took the two quartz crystal clusters we had acquired, along with some of the larger crystals, to our meadow and placed them in different positions, nestled in the dark green ferns, on the stump, joining other stones placed in the Deva sanctuary during its dedication. I took several photos of them in each setting, moving them into different locations where I felt they would be happy. The sun was out that day, the air felt fresh, it was spring and I felt right about what I was doing — seeing the crystals reflecting not only the light, but the feeling I held about these intelligences.

When the processed film came back, I looked for their energy formations. Nothing was obvious, so I turned to the negatives, looking for some subtle energy formations sometimes not seen on the print. Nothing.

Was it because I was expecting the lights? Possible. Was it because the crystals did not choose to open to me that day? Also possible. Was it because the timing wasn't right? Were there reasons unknown to my conscious mind that had to do with information that would be given in the future? Possible, possible.

Another lesson delivered: Have no expectations...

Just shortly before the acquisition of the crystals at the barter fair, I had decided to establish a Deva sanctuary; but when we returned with the crystals and other gemstones, it was apparent that there was much more than one purpose for their acquisition. Not only were there certain crystals that were to be displayed and enjoyed in our home, there were also certain ones that I felt should be outside.

The "right" location for the Deva sanctuary was near the spot where I had first photographed Andrea. It was at the edge of the woods, west of the meadow, where the morning light would play on the trees, the summer sun would be filtered through the pines, and it was out of the usual path of human activity. I put boundary markers on the trees that I felt formed the natural outline of the sanctuary. Using an old stump for many of the stones to rest on, putting some of the larger crystals around the base of it, then standing on the easterly tip of the sanctuary, I offered this special place to the Devas and Nature Spirits as a gesture of love and appreciation. It wasn't until after this short ceremony was completed that I realized the trees marking the boundary of the sanctuary formed the shape of a double-terminated crystal.

Late winter in 1992 brought with it a message from one of the crystal clusters which rested on our coffee table. It wanted to go outside, back to Nature. I moved it to the stump in the Deva sanctuary, allowing it to once again enjoy the snow and rain and wind and sun and the liveliness of the seasons, the elements. I felt good about moving it, and I know it felt good.

Then in early spring, I became very much aware that we had not worked with the rest of our crystals for some time. I got the subtle feeling that they were not as joyful as they were when they first came home with us and took a bath in the cool stream, that they were not fulfilling their purpose in being here, or more likely, they *had* fulfilled it and were now awaiting their next journey. The impressions became stronger. Finally it reached my conscious awareness: They were to be returned to the earth!

I gathered up all the clusters and most of the special stones that had been more like decorations than energy devices, and took them to the Deva sanctuary. As I collected them to be moved to their new location, they appeared to be dull, lifeless, like a child who has been given little love and no touch for a long period of time. As I placed them in the arrangement that seemed right, I was able to directly compare the new arrivals with the cluster that I had taken there during the winter. What a difference! The cluster that had been moved there a month or so prior was sparkling, clear and responsive to my arrival. The ones I placed in the sanctuary "spoke" in unison, telling me how happy they were, now that they were being placed in the arms of Nature once again. This was a timely reminder to pay attention to the subtleties, the little nudgings. That is where *deep* truth is stored.

In the short three years that the Deva sanctuary has existed, one very noticeable change has taken place. The jack pines, which are the dominant species of tree on our land, are being replaced all around the Deva sanctuary with grand fir trees, trees that have a much longer life and grow taller. The jack pines that form the appearance of the double-terminated crystal outlining the Deva sanctuary are dying, or more appropriately, returning to the earth and making room for the fir trees, or some other surprise gift the Devas have in mind. Out of the nine trees that form the outline, five have chosen to provide space for whatever is to come.

Of the various species of trees on our land, the grand fir has been the least prolific of all, and even though there are a few now springing up in other locations on our land, the concentration of grand firs around this very special place is no accident. If one were to compare the density of the firs surrounding the sanctuary with other locations, the concentration would be at least 10 to 20 times greater near the sanctuary.

As I became more and more aware of the concentration of the grand firs, I also sought to make some kind of cosmic sense out of it. I turned to Pamela Chase and Jonathan Pawlik's book *Trees For Healing* (Newcastle Publishing) and found the quote from the Grand Fir Deva more than a little interesting.

"From the time you were very young, you have been taught that it is wrong to express what you are feeling inside. When you do not acknowledge or express painful feelings when they occur, the energy of those feelings remains stored in your subconscious memory, and in the very cells of your body. A current experience can trigger the energy of stored emotions, so that you may not understand why an emotion is present.

"My energies can help you go back in time to the moment when the original experience occurred, so that you can better understand the feelings that were attached to it. I share with you what needs to be healed inside, so that you can then disconnect from the past experience.

"Once you better understand the hidden facets of an issue, my energies can aid you in seeing where change can be instigated instead of saying, "I should have known better or I wouldn't be in this particular state," you learn through me not to judge, but rather to accept what is revealed to you so that you can heal.

"Throughout this process, trust that what you are feeling in any given moment is real to you, and not a product of your imagination. Your emotional body, when you listen to it, gives you the gift of honesty.

"My energies can teach you to value your emotional nature as a way of understanding your spirituality. When you move from the space of fear to one of Unconditional Love through the unfoldment of your emotional being, then you become more receptive to the energies of your spiritual body. Your emotional sensitivity becomes a springboard for your spiritual evolution."

Many years ago, a merchant I was calling on made the astute comment, "You can't catch all the trains," which applies to all of us who want to know more, do more, be like someone else, have someone else's gift, their abilities, their knowledge. Many people have told me, and more have implied, they would like to communicate with Nature Spirits, take photographs like I do, receive verbal messages and have a stronger connection with the unseen intelligences.

The verbal, visual connections are just a part, not the whole, for if a person walks in the woods and feels goosebumps, metaphysical chills, a feeling of wonder, a connection has been made. The trees don't have to speak to each one of us, nor us to them. Their language is not verbal, nor is the language of the Devas and Nature Spirits that work in our gardens, the fairies that joyfully dance in the glade, the animals, domestic or wild, that live in this time and place. It is the *feeling* that is most important, and although the verbal and visual experiences add validity to our dimensional expression, they do not, in themselves, make the process either more or less real, more or less valuable.

This is not to say that we shouldn't attempt to be aware of the communication that I feel is ongoing. A partnership with the Beings of the Earth, the Nature Spirits, the Devas, is very important, and the more we are aware of their existence, and the part that we play in the partnership, the more we will be able to work with them. But I do believe that we can flagellate ourselves for not being aware, for not being completely awake, and this serves to restrain our knowledge that is already within each of us.

As the time release capsule in each human is activated, the information will come, being stimulated into action by various sources; others' teachings, the introduction of certain books or tapes into our lives, or just allowing the information to flow to and through us.

In my recent, personal experience, I am finding more and more information coming through other humans in the form of suggestions, most often being offered to me for reasons the person is not aware of, the person just having a kind of a compulsion to share. And perhaps this has always been the case. But I know I am now more alert to these subtleties, listening now to the insistent quality of the voice, the repetition of the suggestion, the underlying *something* that I can't clearly define.

At an EXPO in Ashland, Oregon, in the spring of 1992, one lady who was visiting my booth asked if I had tried video. I explained that I had purchased a home video camera a couple years prior to that time, but nothing in the way of energy formations had shown up.

"Try it again," she suggested. Then, before leaving the booth, she said, "Be sure to try video." On my mailing list sign-up, she left her name, a happy-face drawing and the message," Try video."

Another visitor at another EXPO asked me if the images show up before I take the picture. I said that they didn't. He then explained that he collected flower essences, and that they sometimes show up for him.

"I think that's wonderful," I said to this large stranger.

"Before you take the pictures, do you ask them to show up?"

I thanked the man for coming into the booth, for in the several years of doing this, I had never *asked* — the most simple, direct method of contact — and I had never done it!

A friend recently suggested that I take one roll of film, ask the beings of a particular dimension to show, then select another dimension and take another roll. This suggestion also has merit.

Whether or not direct, expected results are experienced

by acting on these suggestions — these inclinations — is not as important as putting something into the Universe, creating a movement that will, in some manner, manifest itself.

My choice to become this kind of photographer — a choice made very recently in my life — was made because, during this life, I have leaned toward the logical, left-brain way of doing things, tending to analyze while remaining somewhat skeptical if events don't fit the logical mold. What better way to understand the skeptic's beliefs than to have been one of them — not too long ago. Now, in the words of our friend, Syd, in Lake Almanor, "I'm trying to become illogical."

Much of the time, the urges that I feel, the inward movement that demands a change in the direction of my life, does not provide the clarity that my linear mind would like. But to remove the mystery would take away a lot of the magic, the fun. Right now, my totality is getting this mind/body complex ready for *something*, and I don't have a strong feeling about *what* it is, except it might have something to do with light, or the entire electromagnetic spectrum.

In 1990, I went to the Mind, Body, Spirit and Earth EXPO in Seattle, and experienced some very strange and wonderful things, not all of which are clear to me at this writing. One of the reasons that I went to the EXPO was because Dennis Weaver was going to speak on the environment; but, when I got there, people and lectures appeared from nowhere to lovingly engulf me. I found myself in lecture after lecture asking myself, Why am I here? Some of the lectures had to do with light, the kind you read by, eat by, live by. I sat through, with great interest, a discussion of healing with light, finding myself there more than a little interested, since I am not attracted to the healing disciplines. I even bought a 660 nanometer L.E.D. (red light) device that I thought might be of some help to Mike in relieving some of her physical conditions which cause her discomfort.

Many times I found myself listening to lectures about human relations and other subjects that were not in my arena of interest. Upon my return to Idaho, I received a tape in the mail, a recording of a speech by Richard Hatch at the EXPO, titled, "Acting from the Heart." It was excellent, but I hadn't ordered it, nor — to my knowledge — even left my address with the people who do the recordings and sell the tapes. Where did it come from? Why me, why now, why, why?

The last day of the EXPO, Sunday, I left early, thinking I had better head back to Sandpoint. Less than a block from the exhibit hall, as I was walking toward where I had parked my truck, I experienced the earth tilting, *really* tilting. The sidewalk, fortunately, was wide, probably six or eight feet, and I used it all, staggering first to my right, unable to keep my balance, then to the left and almost into the street. My head was clear, I felt fine, my health is excellent, and there was no earthquake, except, of course, in my personal reality.

I carefully crossed the street toward my truck, decided I had better wait for an aftershock, if one was to come, had a sandwich at a fast food place, then proceeded toward home.

My inner feelings about this personal earthquake has to do with a shifting of energy. Our center of gravity is located in the solar plexus, the energy center of power, and the experience was related to a shift of energy from the solar plexus to the heart, and it happened so suddenly that it actually *threw me off balance!*

After I had been home for a few days, I found myself breathing light. The first of the winter's snow was on the ground, and as I walked outside I could actually feel the light enter my body as it was reflected from the snow. It wasn't like I was visualizing, trying to accomplish something, it was — well, just natural — each molecule receiving life through light, my body seemingly awaiting this experience, my whole being reacting like one hungry for a long-sought-after bit of nourishment. It was astounding, and I found myself going through library books relating to light and the electromagnetic spectrum. I called Kodak to see what wavelengths their film would reproduce, what were the films' parameters. Finally my level of curiosity, decaying with the passage of time, returned to a less piqued state, but awaiting other subtle reminders that "something is going on."

Another incident relating to the electromagnetic spectrum occurred in November 1991, at my second Body, Mind, Spirit and Earth EXPO. I never dreamed, when I phoned for a program, that I would become an exhibitor.

When the program arrived, I was thrilled to see that Dorothy Maclean of Findhorn Garden fame was to appear as a part of a three-hour special. I really wanted to meet that lady; but, as a visitor at the EXPO, I would be reluctant to walk up to her and say, "By the way, I take photographs of the Nature Spirits you communicate with." This would be too weird; there had to be a better way to make contact.

On the back of the program from the EXPO, printed diagonally, was the statement, "Exhibitors: Limited booth space is still available."

"Booth Space?" I muttered to myself, "Exhibitor?" I called, committed to booth space, was allocated 45 minutes for a personal presentation in which to show my slides to anyone who wanted to attend, and had the wonderful experience of sharing my photographs with many interested, and interesting, persons.

On the second day of the EXPO, a young couple entered my booth, asked me about the photographs and posters I had on display, how I was able to do it, how it came about, how long I had been doing it — the normal and usual questions I am asked. The man asked most of the questions, and the more we talked, the more I found I was in harmony with this person, this stranger with the gentle, sincere manner. Just before they left the booth, he explained that he was Kurt Mann, the director and producer of the video, *Opening Doors Within*. The video that was to be shown during the three-hour Findhorn special. I explained to Kurt that the very reason I was in the EXPO as an exhibitor was to meet Dorothy Maclean. He offered to introduce me.

When Kurt introduced me, I felt just a little foolish explaining to this fine, down-to-earth person that I thought the reason I came to the EXPO was to connect with her. But I invited her to stop by the booth when she had time, so we might talk. It shouldn't have been a surprise to me by now to *expect* the unexpected. She, being a busy woman, and — I sensed — not drawn to the New Age goings-on at the EXPO, chose not to come by the booth. It was late on Sunday that I realized the connection with her was *not* the reason I was at the EXPO — it was the networking and the connection with Kurt Mann, and the subsequent discussion we had relating to the medium of video and electromagnetic energy.

There was a whole lot of synchronicity going on during this small act in the play of life. First, I called EXPO for a program, learned that Dorothy Maclean would be there, then learning of the exhibit space availability, Kurt Mann stopping by the booth, his introduction of Dorothy to me, and our subsequent discussion of electromagnetic gestalts.

Kurt and I were definitely tuned into the same frequencies, which was made more evident to me the next morning as I helped him arrange chairs for the capacity crowd that would be in attendance for the three-hour special. As he set up the presentation equipment, he pushed the "play" button on the projector, and *before the first image was shown on the screen*, when the first chord of music was played, I told Kurt I had to have a copy of the video. Not exactly *logical.*

After the three-hour presentation, when Kurt stopped by my booth once again, we discussed many things, and during our conversation I asked him if everyone on the set was in harmony with what was being done to bring this video into being.

His reply was, "It was a spiritual experience for everyone involved."

I then explained to Kurt why I felt we are sometimes drawn so strongly to a film, like I was to his, realizing as I spoke that the impact of videos goes far beyond the audio and visual aspects of the film. We project electromagnetic energy from our bodies all the time, which is scientifically proven by Kirlian photography, which shows human and plant (and probably animal) auras. And as we (unconsciously) project this vibration, our collective energies are then combined into an electromagnetic gestalt, almost like a separate entity, and its essence becomes impressed on the tape, since the tape is also electromagnetic.

So, when the viewers are exposed to this magnetic source, and providing their vibrational frequencies are in harmony with the tape's frequencies, there is a drawing, a feeling that something more than audio and video are a part of this tape's composition. Kurt said it made absolute good sense to him.

It was then that I knew *why* I had come to Seattle. It was not to exhibit, it was not to meet Dorothy Maclean as I had thought, but to meet Kurt so we could have this discussion; his presence and interaction became a catalyst for the birth of this concept into our/my conscious awareness.

Shortly after I returned home, I meditated for the first time in quite a long while, and during meditation I received the thought that the origin of the beings in my photographs is electromagnetic. The word "origin" is underscored in my mind, which could mean that the beings are electromagnetic, and, as their energies are impressed upon the film, the electromagnetic vibrations blend with the chemical emulsions, but leave the electromagnetic source intact This explains why certain people are drawn to certain photographs; the observer's vibrational pattern is in phase or harmonically resonant with the energies in the photograph. This is also the reason why some who are sensitive can "read" the photographs, pick up sometimes subtle emanations, translate these impulses to thoughts and verbalize or write them, commonly referred to as channeling.

What we cannot understand, we often negate; what we cannot see, we selectively disbelieve. I say selectively because there are many things that we accept without seeing, and there are other things we do not accept because they cannot be proven. No one has seen oxygen or wind. Do they, therefore, *not* exist? How about television waves, radio waves, X-rays, gamma rays, ozone, carbon dioxide, nitrogen, memory, thought, love? If we accept these things without seeing them, why, then, do we not fully accept the possibility of intelligences and our own greater potential, even though unseen?

My suggestion, relating to the invisible Nature Spirits and other multidimensional beings, is that we equate intelligence with the *human* mind, or at least a physical brain, and since these intelligences are not remotely human, our logical mind steps in and tells us that there is no such thing as invisible intelligence, since intelligence needs a physical body. Our left brain judges these things to be unreal; the voice we hear, the visions we see, the feelings we get, are — in some strange way — relegated to "one of those things."

I am still in awe that I can photograph unseen energies, that I have the ability and the responsibility to act as a bridge between other realities and our own, and that — at a completely different level — I am fully aware of what I am doing but am unable, at this writing, to bring all the facts into the light of conscious awareness. I am, however, learning to not expect, not to try, not to be disappointed, to just let things flow. My left brain, which I have encouraged to be dominant throughout my business life, objects to not understanding the process, wants to be able to put the whole thing into a neat file and store it away, readily accessible for future use, if needed. It would like to categorize all the data, classify, separate, document; but at the same time my right brain is very relaxed about the whole thing, telling me, "There is nothing to prove, there is nothing that has to be explained in logical, linear terms, there is nothing that is important about the process. It is the end result — the knowledge that we are indeed in communication with other realities and, as we lift the veils from our minds, the view will be spectacularly clear."

I have come to realize that my responsibility is to just lift one corner of the veil in order to assist in elevating awareness. It is all part of the process, part of our growth and, for some reason, this decade is right and this body/mind complex is right for the job. It's kind of a miracle.

The beings you have been introduced to in this book in the form of photographs and stories are real; they are not imagined. They exist in a non-physical sense, just as you and I exist in a non-physical *and* physical sense.

We limit ourselves daily by believing that what is seen in the mirror is all there is, that where our body ends is where we end. It is important that we understand a greater truth, that our existence is primarily in the spiritual and secondarily in the physical — not the other way around — and that we all possess gifts that are of immeasurable value to others, to ourselves and to the Universe.

What talent or gift do you, the reader, own? What ability do you have this very moment that is not being fully actualized? What subtle movements in your being are telling you to pay attention, to listen to your heart, your body, your intuition, guiding you — through gentle reminders in your dreams or your waking-up time, your day-dreams, the synchronicity of events — to the knowledge that you have a wealth of untapped potential lying just beneath the surface, waiting to be born, to be put into action?

I would suggest that the greatest gifts need no fanfare, no spectacular fireworks display, to become important. For who or what can dictate importance — except the heart?

I have come to accept, through the ongoing synchronicity of events, some of which are outlined in this book, that the greatest miracles in our lives can be found in the subtleties, the "coincidences," the "accidental happenings" of everyday existence on this planet, and that as we pay attention, realizing that we are all co-creators in this play of life — that we are the writers, the directors, the actors. Then every moment of the day becomes the big event, the gift, showing us in unmistakable terms that, behind the veil, we are all ... Beings of Light.

—*A Gift From the Author*—

Select any one of the *Beings of Light* images shown in this book, and a beautiful, full-color note card will be mailed to you absolutely free, along with a current listing of other cards.

Simply complete a copy of the following, and mail to the address shown below.

Image selected (page number) _____

Name:_____

Address:_____

City, State, Zip: _____

Mail this request to:

Orin Bridges
P.O. Box 11
Dover, ID 83825

—About the Author—

Born and raised in the Midwest, Orin Bridges and his family moved to California in the early 1950s, where he was employed in the electronics field as a sales representative, became branch manager of a national firm in Los Angeles, then entered real estate to become involved in real estate exchanging and financial planning. He later wrote and conducted real estate seminars on creative uses of mortgages and trust deeds, but it was not until after his "retirement" that he found his real connection with Nature.

Since that time, Bridges' determination to become more self-sufficient, to conserve the earth's resources, led him to the design and construction of a solar-powered home in north Idaho, where he and his wife now live. It was there that the surprise gift of photographing Beings of Light was discovered.

The surplus electricity generated by photovoltaic panels on the roof of the Bridges' home is now being used to charge the batteries in a vehicle Orin converted from a gasoline powered to electric powered, and is used for energy-free, pollution-free commuting.

Photographing Beings of Light
Images of Nature and Beyond

by Orin Bridges

Order Form

For additional copies of *Photographing Beings of Light*, telephone TOLL FREE 1-800-356-9315. MasterCard/Visa accepted.

To order *Photographing Beings of Light* directly from the publisher, send your check or money order to Rainbow Books, Inc., Order Dept., P. O. Box 430, Highland City, FL 33846-0430.

Trade Softcover — $14.95 plus $3.00 shipping and handling ($17.95 postpaid).

For QUANTITY PURCHASES, telephone Rainbow Books, Inc. (813) 648-4420 or write to The Publisher, Rainbow Books, Inc., P. O. Box 430, Highland City, FL 33846 0430.